NURSING MOTHER, WORKING MOTHER

NURSING MOTHER, WORKING MOTHER

THE ESSENTIAL GUIDE FOR BREASTFEEDING AND STAYING CLOSE TO YOUR BABY AFTER YOU RETURN TO WORK

GALE PRYOR

THE HARVARD COMMON PRESS
Boston, Massachusetts

The Harvard Common Press
535 Albany Street
Boston, Massachusetts 02118

Printed in the United States of America
Printed on acid-free paper

Library of Congress Cataloging-in-Publication Data

Pryor, Gale.
Nursing mother, working mother : the essential guide for
breastfeeding and staying close to your baby after you return
to work / Gale Pryor.
p.   cm.
Includes bibliographical references and index.
ISBN 1-55832-116-0 (cloth). — ISBN 1-55832-117-9 (paper)
1. Breast feeding—Popular works.   2. Working mothers.   I. Title.
RJ216.P768   1997
649'.33—dc21   96-46491

Cover design by Kathleen Herlihy-Paoli, Inkstone Design
Text design by Norman Sevigny, Irving Perkins Associates
Cover photograph © Ariel Skelley/The Stock Market
Illustrations by Meryl Brenner

Special bulk-order discounts are available on this and other
Harvard Common Press books. Companies and organizations may
purchase books for premiums or for resale, or may arrange
a custom edition, by contacting the Marketing Director
at the address above.

10 9 8 7 6 5 4 3 2 1

For my boys: Kolya, Max, Wylie, and . . .

CONTENTS

ACKNOWLEDGMENTS

This book began taking shape nine years ago, when I returned to work following the birth of my first son, Max. In a new city far from family, alone among my friends in having become a mother, unique among my coworkers in attempting to combine mothering and working, I was nearly overwhelmed by anxiety and strain. The support of experienced mothers and friends in the same stage of life would have made everything so much easier.

At the very least, a book that addressed my situation, including both the practical problems to which I was devising answers and the emotional events I was weathering, would have helped a great deal. Now, having authored that wished-for book, I know that having a baby and writing a book share much in common. In particular, friends and family make the job so much easier.

Neither my sons nor this book would have been possible without the help of my best friend and husband, Karl Leabo. His encouragement as I spent hours upon hours at the computer, his gift of a beautiful desk, his endless patience at living with piles of papers, boxes of books, and inkstains on the bed sheets whenever I fell asleep while underlining a reference were all major contributions to the completion of the writing. The imaginative weekend expeditions on which he took our sons, while I stayed home to write, vastly improved what could have been a dreary year for them. These sons, marvelous Max and wonderful Wylie, deserve thanks as well. They have been my inspiration, my teachers, and my rewards throughout the hard work of becoming a mother and a writer.

This book also came to be because of my mother, Karen Pryor. Writer, biologist, behaviorist, breastfeeding expert, dolphin researcher, dog guru, keynote speaker, grandmother, birdwatcher, botanist, carpenter, needlepointer, mountain climber, and museum-goer, she has shown me that the world is an endlessly fascinating place—all of it worth learning and writing about. Her encouragement and editorial comments fueled me through a long year of writing. She shall continue to inspire me all my life.

Three years ago, vaguely pondering the idea of this book, I attended a regional La Leche League (LLL) Conference. After a morning of seminars, during which I realized that this conference was in every way like the professional seminars I had attended in the course of my career except that a multitude of babies and children were present, I arrived for the luncheon in the hotel ballroom. Looking around for an empty seat, and finding one at a table of strangers, I sat down next to Gerry Anne Dubis. A La Leche League leader from New Hampshire, Gerry Anne, as luck would have it, had helped countless working mothers to nurse their babies. By the time dessert was served, Gerry Anne and I were planning our own seminar to be given at the following LLL conference. Later she donated hours (including a particularly pleasant day at a sidewalk cafe in Portsmouth, New Hampshire) to updating and advising me and examining the text of the book for inaccuracies; her experience and expertise are laced throughout these chapters. Her energy, good humor, and kindness kept me going.

I am especially grateful as well to Kittie Frantz, pediatric nurse practitioner and professor of lactation at the University of Southern California Medical School, who provided a thoughtful review of the manuscript, invaluable expertise, and resources, including her astonishingly complete *Breastfeeding Product Guide*.

Linda Ziedrich's meticulous editing also reassured me that this book would be the best it could be.

I owe special thanks, too, to the many mothers who corresponded with me across the Internet, sharing their concerns and solutions. They are quoted throughout the book, but remain unnamed because so often they signed their e-mail with only their cyberspace names. Women who participated in computer forums and message boards about attachment parenting and working mothers also contributed to this book; I read their dialogues with fascination.

Judith Ravel and Maurice Wakeman, grandparents extraordinaire, kept my family in good company and well fed while I toiled. Maurice taught me, as he did hundreds of parents in his pediatric practice, that all a parent really needs is confidence. He did not live to see this book's publication, and we miss him sorely.

Many others provided inspiration and practical help: Susan Shulman Polit and Mary Jane Daly, neighbors, fellow moms, incisive intellects, and friends forever, became my sounding boards in exchange for cups of tea. Deborah Sloan, Susan Halperin, and the other women of Candlewick Press, all shining examples of dedicated professionals who have kept their jobs from coming between their children and themselves, shared their insights and experiences and cheered me through the publishing process from contract to reviews. Meryl Brenner, also a Candlewick colleague and mom, brought her considerable talents and her patient nature to the job of illustrator. Wendy Wakeman Staschke and baby Maurice spent an afternoon happily nursing in whatever position I requested while Mary Gunn Wakeman snapped photos. David Jaffe made the inestimably valuable gift of a laptop computer, which enabled me to travel with my family without having to stop work on the book. To them and the many others who have shared their lives and enthusiasm with me, I offer my thanks.

A NOTE ABOUT THE TERM
WORKING MOTHER

As anyone who has ever raised a child knows full well, all mothers are working mothers. Mothers with jobs heartily agree that the work they do at home is usually more physically exhausting and mentally taxing than the work they do for pay. Unfortunately, our language does not provide a useful and accurate term for those mothers who have major responsibilities outside the family as well as within it. The term *employed mothers* excludes both mothers who are employers and mothers who are students. *Working mothers* may seem to slight women without jobs, but it is all we are left with. Although written with the understanding that mothering requires as much effort and skill as any paid job, this book is about the challenge of combining dual social roles.

PREFACE

"I am going back to work after the baby is born."

The necessity of returning to work is one of the most common reasons that women decide against breastfeeding. And yet breastfeeding can be one of the best things a working mother ever did for herself or her baby.

In 1987, a few weeks before giving birth to my first child, I told my obstetrician that I planned to breastfeed even though I would be returning to work after a two-month maternity leave. She said that I probably would be unable to pump enough milk to feed the baby during our separations, and that the baby probably wouldn't take a bottle, anyway. The day-care provider I'd chosen told me she didn't usually accept breastfed babies into her home because she didn't like keeping breast milk in her refrigerator. My boss turned pale and averted his eyes when I mentioned that I would need 20 minutes twice a day to pump my milk. He then denied me an extra, third month of maternity leave. Even my always supportive husband worried that I would be too exhausted to breastfeed.

Fortunately, about thirty years before, my mother, Karen Pryor, had breastfed my two brothers and me. She nursed us in a time when breastfeeding was an oddity, unfashionable and discouraged. She nursed despite being told that she couldn't breastfeed because all three of her children had been born by cesarean section (I still haven't figured out the reason for that). Rather than accepting the doctor's decision and taking up the bottle, she got mad. She went to the library and read. She traveled to talk with other breastfeeding mothers. She learned all she could about breastfeeding, and she put it in a book, *Nursing Your Baby.* Now in its third edition, her book has sold more than a million copies over twenty years, and it has helped mothers around the world joyfully nurse their babies.

Yet nearly thirty years after my mother bucked our culture's prejudice against breastfeeding, I was up against it in a new, subtler form. I began to see that, in our culture, the involved mothering that breastfeeding signifies was considered incompatible with a commitment to one's career. If I were to stay in a world in which success was modeled on men's lives, I was not expected also to seek success in a traditionally feminine way. Make your choice, said our society, children or career, mother or star employee, woman or man-woman.

So I did what my mother would have done. I got mad. I had just begun my career in a field that I loved, and I did not want to quit now. And I was determined to nurse my baby until he weaned himself. Eight weeks after my son Max was born, I returned to full-time work, pumping twice a day and nursing in the evenings, nights, and early mornings, and on the weekends. Max weaned himself at 18 months, while I was away on a three-day business trip.

I had proved my obstetrician wrong, and yet I found that my new role as mother continued to conflict with my life at work. I discovered that chatting about babies while waiting for a meeting to begin was unprofessional (whereas discussing the previous night's baseball game was not). My unwillingness to fly to Chicago at the drop of a hat was taken as evidence of a lack of commitment. I no longer stayed at work a minute past five o' clock, but rushed to the elevators and home to my baby, shrugging off thoughts of how my behavior was affecting my image as a hard worker. I split my life in two as I took on two incompatible identities. I felt terribly torn between excelling at the job I loved and learning this new, equally compelling job of motherhood.

Breastfeeding, however, far from becoming an additional source of stress, relieved my anxieties. My confidence suddenly shaken in all the areas I once felt so sure in, I knew that in this one function, nurturing my child, I was doing fine. Breastfeeding reassured me that, even though Max spent much of the day with a babysitter he adored, I was irreplaceable to him. Only I could offer him a warm breast full of sweet milk. At the end of each day, when I nursed him before heading home from the sitter's house, there was no "getting to know you again" adjustment period. We were immediately a couple, instantly and completely in tune with one another.

There were myriad other benefits to Max and to me. Breastfeeding turned out to be more convenient than bottle feeding, a blessing considering my demanding schedule. Breastfeeding was relaxing, too. As soon as my milk let down, I found it difficult to remember what had vexed me so at the office that day, and I came to rely on the calm that always followed a peaceful nursing. Breastfeeding also helped me to focus on Max, and to make the most of my precious time with him. His fingers toying with the buttons on my blouse, his bright eyes looking up, and his quick smile that sent milk dribbling down his cheek as he nursed swept away worries about getting dinner made and laundry done. If I had artificially fed Max, there would have been many a night when I might have propped him up with a bottle "just for a minute" while I put a pot on the stove or a load in the washing machine. Breastfeeding helped me remember that what my baby needed most of all was me.

Looking back, I realize that continuing to breastfeed while working tied the two halves of my life together and helped me make sense of myself as a mother. Breastfeeding gave my baby the best beginning, and also guided my first steps as his mother. The gentle, intuitive intimacy between a breastfed baby and his mother provided me with a blueprint for parenting my child long after weaning.

I found, too, that at work I could draw on the confidence I had acquired by successfully nursing my baby. I gained perspective on matters that once riled me. I began to extend to the world at large the calm acceptance, the warm receptivity, that I had learned through breastfeeding.

Most importantly, however, continuing to breastfeed while working kept me from submerging the mother I had become beneath the driven, working person I had long been. Breastfeeding helped me to become aware of, and then to resist, the pressure to pretend for eight hours a day that no baby was at home competing with the business for my time and devotion. Breastfeeding was my declaration that I could get the job done as a woman rather than as a man.

I have since watched as so many women, ceding to cultural pressure, accept the premise that employees do not have private lives, children do not have daily needs, and home and work are two separate spheres that must never come in contact with each other. This living in two separate worlds at once, while obligated to meet the competing demands of each, is, I believe, the source of overwhelming stress for employed mothers.

I hope that this book will help you combine your working life and your home life, through breastfeeding and sensitive parenting, to form a unity between yourself as a mother and the person you are on the job. I hope it will help you learn not to balance but to *blend* the two sides of your life, so that you may simultaneously raise your child, enjoy your work, and, perhaps, serve as an example to others that raising children is not a personal hobby, but a joyful responsibility that we must all take on together.

NURSING MOTHER, WORKING MOTHER

CHAPTER ONE

BONDING, BREASTFEEDING, AND THE WORKING MOTHER

"I can't take my eyes off my baby. She's perfect."

Becoming a mother is an experience full of surprises. The most astonishing surprise of all may be the intensity of your feelings for your new baby. Before your baby is born, you may have trouble imagining your life with a baby in it. After your baby is born, though, you can't imagine life without this new, extraordinary person. Becoming a mother is an experience that changes you forever.

The quality of the experience varies from woman to woman. For a few, the first weeks and months of motherhood seem enchanted. For others, this is a period of transition and adjustment in which the enchantment of mothering occurs only gradually. In either case, returning to work may become suddenly inconceivable for a mother once she falls in love with her new child. Many a pregnant woman never imagines how hard it will be to leave her baby.

How Mothers and Babies Bond

The first moments of motherhood have always fascinated observers of human behavior. In studying mothers and their newborns, researchers have identified a universal, elegant interplay that sparks the lifelong bond between mothers and their children.

A bond between any two people, including a mother and baby, develops and deepens over time. Babies, however, arrive in the world designed to initiate and establish that bond. Able to see, hear, smell, and feel with far more clarity than one might assume, newborns use their amazing innate abilities to make their parents want to care for them, want to help them grow and thrive. Your baby's first developmental task, one for which she has abundant talent, is to make you fall head over heels in love with her.

New mothers also behave in ways that seem to be instinctive. We almost always touch our newborns in the same way, first with our fingertips, then with the palms of our hands, moving from their extremities to their tummies and backs and lastly to their faces. We tend to hold our babies in what researchers call the *en face* position, so that our faces are 8 to 12 inches from our babies' faces, which happens to be the distance in which newborn eyes can most easily focus. We usually have an intense desire to make eye-to-eye contact with our babies, and we find their returned gaze immensely gratifying. We speak to our babies in high, soft voices reserved especially for them. And our babies respond to our touch, our gaze, our voice, and even our scent in myriad, enchanting ways that lead us to touch them, gaze at them, and speak to them ever more in a cycle of interactions that over time create a richly layered mother-child relationship.

John Kennell and Marshall Klaus, the pioneering researchers in mother-infant bonding, have described this intricate, instinctive pattern of interactions as "a fail-safe system that is over-determined to ensure the proximity of mother and child." The deep attachment arising from your natural interactions with your baby will allow you to meet his needs intuitively—and will help him to feel secure whenever he is close to you. Even if you and your newborn must be separated for a time just after birth—if one of you becomes ill, for example—your dance of attachment will continue, though at a slower tempo. And even if you are so overwhelmed with exhaustion, worry, or other feelings that falling in love must wait, you and your baby will, finally, become deeply bonded when you are ready. Once this happens, you

Mothers have an intense desire to make eye-to-eye contact with their babies. It's just one part of a collection of bonding behaviors exhibited by both mothers and babies.

will have formed the first strong strand of a lifelong bond that cannot easily be broken.

The Role of Breastfeeding in Bonding

Breastfeeding usually plays an integral role in forming the deep attachment between mother and baby. Bottle-feeding mothers, of course, can also be securely attached to their babies. There are many tools in the attachment kit; breastfeeding is but one. It is, however, an extraordinarily powerful one.

Breastfeeding is designed by nature to ensure maternal-infant interaction and closeness. If done without schedules or other restrictions, breastfeeding guarantees that you and your baby will be in close physical contact 8 to 18 times in every 24 hours. In fact, nursing mothers tend to be with their infants altogether more than other mothers. In the first 10 days after birth, nursing mothers hold their babies more than bottle-feeding mothers, even when they are not nursing. They rock their babies more, speak to their babies more, and are more likely to sleep with their babies. In Western society many women never hold a newborn until they give birth to their own, yet this frequent skin-to-skin contact and interaction soon make up for even a complete lack of familiarity with babies. The mother who immerses herself in her newborn, breastfeeding frequently and without restrictions, quickly learns to read her baby's cues and to trust her own instincts. She extends the gentle give-and-take, the empathy, and the commitment of breastfeeding into the rest of her mothering. Nursing her baby provides her with a blueprint for sensitive parenting in the years to come.

Nursing couples need each other physically and emotionally. The baby, of course, has a physical need for milk. As scientists have amply documented, breast milk benefits every system in a baby's body. Breast-feeding offers protection against allergies and respiratory infections, and perhaps obesity. Breastfeeding improves vision and oral development; breastfed babies have fewer ear infections; breast milk is better for the cardiovascular system and kidneys; and babies' intestinal immunity is enhanced by human milk. Juvenile diabetes is less common among breastfed than bottle-fed babies. Breastfeeding enhances a baby's cognitive development, partially because it allows the baby more control in feeding—and the ability to control one's own actions appears to be essential in human development. The composition of breast milk, too, appears to support optimal brain development. Indeed, recent studies have found that children fed mother's milk as babies have higher IQs, on average, than those fed formula.

And, of course, a baby's emotional need for love and reassurance is just as strong as her physical need for milk. Whereas most formula-fed babies are soon taught to hold their own bottles, the breastfed baby is always held by her mother for feedings. A breastfed baby enjoys not only the comfort of the warm breast, but caressing, rocking, and eye contact before, during, and after feedings. With all her senses, she drinks in her mother's love.

The mother, in turn, has a physical need for the baby to take the milk from her breasts. The let-down of milk is relieving, satisfying, like a drink of water when one is thirsty. When your newborn begins to suck at your breast, or even just to mouth your nipple, the hormone oxytocin is released in your body, hastening the contraction of your uterus and inducing the let-down or milk-ejection reflex, which begins your milk flow. Called "the love hormone" because it is also produced during sexual intercourse and birth, oxytocin brings on a sudden feeling of contentment and pleasure as you breastfeed your baby. In this way you and your baby become a happy team at feedings, each amply rewarded by the other for her efforts.

The Confident Parent

Successful breastfeeding not only tends to produce healthy, happy babies, it also creates confident mothers. Marianne Neifert, a pediatrician and mother of five, saw this in her practice. "I began to recognize the impact of early parenting experiences, such as breastfeeding, on long-term parental competency. A woman who received necessary support and information, which enabled her to breastfeed as long as she had planned, tended to look back on her experience with pride and satisfaction. Her confidence radiated to other areas of mothering, and she viewed herself as a competent and successful parent."

> *"Breastfeeding nudges other aspects of maternal behavior."*
>
> —NILES NEWTON

Breastfeeding's gift of confidence comes as you nurture your baby with your own body and mind. Parents who use formula often rely completely on manufacturers' and doctors' advice, and so develop little faith in their own judgment. And, whereas a breastfeeding mother generally leaves milk composition, temperature, cleanliness, and intake to nature, for the formula-feeding parent these are all subjects for worry and argument, which further erode her confidence.

Parenting styles differ enormously from family to family, and many different kinds of families produce wonderful children. Whatever their parenting style, though, mothers and fathers who are confident in themselves as parents tend to raise equally self-assured children. These parents not only teach self-esteem by modeling it, but because they are self-confident they are also empathetic. They respond to their children's needs, and thereby help their children to feel secure, trusting, and confident in themselves and their world.

Far more valuable than advice from relatives, friends, or experts is the knowledge *within* you that you are completely capable of caring for and raising your new baby. Bruno Bettelheim, the child psychologist, writes in *A Good Enough Parent* that "acting on the recommendations of others cannot evoke in us the feelings of confirmation that well up in us only when we have understood *on our own,* in *our own ways,* what is involved in a particular situation, and what we can therefore do about it." Successful breastfeeding kindles these "feelings of confirmation," for the breastfeeding mother knows in her heart that she can nurture her child well.

Breastfeeding, in short, is much more than a feeding method. Beyond providing perfect nutrition at every stage of your baby's growth, breastfeeding is a language, subtle and intimate, between you and your baby, as well as a proud and marvelous expression of your unique abilities as a woman. When you return to work, breastfeeding will ensure that the bond between you and your baby cannot be weakened by your frequent separations.

The Risks of Working to Bonding

Bonding usually proceeds without our thinking about it much. We get pregnant, we give birth, we fall in love with our babies, we decide to breastfeed, we become mothers in tune with our babies. Voilà. We have accomplished one of life's major transitions, becoming a mother. Unless we don't.

Sometimes women don't fully traverse the divide between childless woman and mother. They have babies, but they resist the bone-deep commitment that comes with motherhood. After all, becoming a mother is a frightening, gigantic leap into a new, all-encompassing stage of life. Motherhood threatens to submerge both accomplishments of the past and goals of the future, as well as one's present sense of self. The fear of losing oneself in its flood waters is entirely normal.

Besides, in American culture today, motherhood receives scant respect, especially among high-achievers. If your self-respect comes mainly from your success at work, especially if that work is competitive and pressured, reentering the world with *mother* suddenly attached to your identity can be dismaying, to say the least. Despite the impressive diplomacy and managerial skills with which motherhood endows women, the business world holds mothers in suspicion. We are widely suspected of not being truly committed to our jobs and our employers—and any child-related activity that intrudes upon our work simply confirms that suspicion. In addition, mothers are stereotyped as passive (or patient), noncompetitive (or cooperative), emotional (or sensitive), and irrational (or intuitive)—traits deemed incompatible with the traditionally masculine image of a successful professional.

Women first broke into male fields by disproving feminine stereotypes and by proving that they could do the work as well, *and in the same way,* as men. In the 1970s and 1980s, women edging into the corporate world wore outfits that replicated men's business suits except that the bottom half ended in one hem rather than two. They often avoided having traditionally feminine hobbies and traits. They strived to prove they could be at least as tough, and work at least as long, as any man. Entry into the world of men required, as much as possible, *being* a man. If women wanted equal opportunities, they had to adhere to the existing norms of the workplace—and more often than not, they still have to.

No doubt becoming mock-men was a necessary step in the effort to open doors for women. Many women who now hold high positions in U.S. corporations or in academia forfeited having children and participating in other activities that might have cast them in traditionally feminine roles and therefore might have interfered with their climb up the ladder. Women who did have children behaved at work almost as if their children did not exist—and many working women still feel pressured to do the same. One attorney just back from a three-month maternity leave says, "I'm working very hard to reestablish myself as a lawyer, not a mommy. It's gotten to the point where I almost refuse to talk about the baby in the office." *Breaking the Glass Ceiling,* a study of executive women published in 1992, advises, "For women, it is more important that they visibly limit their family life and personal relationships to convince others that they are committed. . . . The obvious solution for women who want to demonstrate their commitment to the corporation and thereby earn a chance for advancement into the executive suite is to give up everything else, including a family."

Without diminishing those brave and determined women who broke new ground for all of us, I must say that it would be a bizarre and backward success story if feminism's final chapter were about women becoming, for all intents and purposes, men. Surely feminism's triumph will come when women can work in any field they choose without having to sacrifice all the joys or avoid the responsibilities that come with being woman. Will not our society be a better one when mothers can openly nurture their children without risking their careers—when we are able to embrace motherhood without apology? Certainly the lives of children will be improved.

The result of our social revolution is that new mothers returning to their working worlds today are confronted with a culture that doesn't quite know what to do with them. The general confusion about roles and images compounds the personal challenge of changing from working woman into working mother. A woman might logically resist the transition altogether, and continue living her life as if having a baby has had little if any impact on it. In this way she attempts to circumvent the conflict between work and motherhood. Unfortunately, she might find that in the process a distance, an unfamiliarity and mutual discomfort, comes between her and her baby.

This distancing begins in the hospital. A new mother may choose to bottle-feed because she believes that her return to work will require her to wean early anyway. She may believe that formula is just as good for her baby as breast milk and a lot more convenient. She may have been told that a few weeks of nursing are no better than none, or that once she starts breastfeeding she will never get the baby to take a bottle. She may even believe that returning to work will be easier for both her and her baby if she does not allow her baby to become completely dependent on her now. If she wants to try breastfeeding, she might ask the nurses to teach her to use a breast pump even before her milk comes in, for she is focusing on the day she'll return to work.

This new mother may accept the nurses' advice to leave her baby in the nursery except at feeding times so that she herself can get some rest. If she allows the maternity ward staff to care for her newborn, she leaves the hospital with the sense that she and her baby barely know each other.

At home, she begins caring for her baby in ways she hopes will promote "independence." She hopes to have her baby sleeping through the night before her first day back at work, even if this means letting him "cry it out." Her primary goal during her maternity leave is to hire a satisfactory babysitter or to find an opening in a day-care home or center. She may even hire a professional baby nurse to help out until she can find a long-term caregiver. She may take advice like that offered by a guide for career women written in the 1980s, which encourages mothers to "make the most of their maternity leaves" by "calling the office at 10:00 A.M. and 4:00 P.M. every day and going to the office once a week for key meetings." In short, she focuses on the overwhelming management job of combining motherhood with her working life—rather than on becoming her baby's mother.

When her maternity leave is over and this mother is back at work, the hours there seem comfortingly familiar, unlike the time she spends with the little stranger at home. At work the mother's activities are well organized. She can begin and complete a task without interruption. Her work has tangible results. She chats with other adults about interesting things. She avoids chatting about her baby or "mommy" things because she feels she must reestablish her professional image. Pictures of her baby are limited to one or two discreet frames on her desk.

If she is still breastfeeding at all, this mother may give pumping a try, but she quickly finds that she doesn't get much milk with the pump she picked up at the pharmacy. Her milk seems to be drying up anyway, and her baby really does seem to prefer the bottle. She soon gives up the idea of pumping and, shortly afterward, of nursing as well. She may be relieved or she may feel a bit blue about this, but everyone (her doctor, other working mothers, and her relatives) had told her that this would probably happen.

At home, the skills that make her a star at work seem no help in her role as a parent. She grows increasingly dependent on her caregiver's child-care advice, and she begins to feel that perhaps she is just not temperamentally suited to this mothering business. Perhaps, she thinks, it's better to delegate her child's care to professionals. As one mother declares, "I do not regret working, and here's why: (1) I am providing my son with a role model, showing that adults need to work and that women work as well as men, and (2) I am not a 'professional' child rearer, and I want only the best for my baby." Although this mother surely loves her baby as deeply as any other parent does, she does not trust or respect herself as a mother. And the admiration she receives from her professional associates and the rest of society—for joining the ranks of those amazing superwomen, able to "do it all" without a hair out of place—confirms her decision to delegate child rearing.

Unseen is the distance that may be developing between a baby and the mother who lacks confidence in her own abilities to nurture her baby—a distance that is good for neither mother nor baby, but that enables her life to proceed more or less as though a child had never entered the picture. Her baby is growing and developing as he is designed to do, but she is not developing as his mother. She finds it hard to understand why he cries and how to calm him. As he becomes a toddler, they may lock horns frequently as she searches for solutions from friends and experts to the problem of raising her "difficult child." She and her child love each other deeply, but they are not in harmony.

The problem with returning to work after a baby is born is not so much the hours a mother and baby are apart, but that working can cause their lives to run on separate tracks. Working, especially at a job that demands a mother's heart and mind as well as her time, can lead a woman to live two concurrent, incompatible lives. But it is awfully hard to have two separate and yet completely equal priorities. The strain of switching from one role to the other may eventually cause one life to dominate the other. For some women life with the baby dominates, and work goes on at a slower pace or even stops altogether for a few years. For other women work life dominates, and being a baby's mother takes second place. Such a woman stops developing as a mother and becomes emotionally distanced from her baby.

Child-development specialists are concerned about the trend among women to put work before baby. According to Dr. Michael Bulmash, a clinical psychologist in Stamford, Connecticut, "Women have become increasingly uncomfortable in the role of nurturer." The social pressures we face "have created a generation of mothers who are losing their natural ability to pick up on cues and signals from their children."

We need to resist the pressures to surrender or minimize our roles as nurturers. You *can* stay close to your baby, despite the demands of your job, by finding ways, such as breastfeeding, that will help you to develop as a mother.

> *Working outside your home does not mean that you will inevitably be less in tune with your baby than an at-home mother. With awareness and understanding, you can erase the risk of this happening.*

To minimize the risk of alienation between mothers and babies in general, we must change our culture's views of working and mothering. Gunn Johansson, a professor of work psychology at the University of Stockholm, compared the lives of female managers in Sweden and the former West Germany. Although the two societies are similar in many ways, Sweden provides a broad range of benefits, including extended maternity leaves and high-quality child care, to all its families. In Sweden, the study reveals, most of the female managers have at least two children; in Germany, most are single women with no children. German women feel they must forsake family for work, Johansson concludes, whereas Swedish women consider it their right to combine the two roles.

Here in the United States, in the current era of "down-sized" government, women's choices depend more on the goodwill of private corporations than on federal policies. The pressures on American women to further their careers by forsaking their families comes primarily from corporate culture. How easily you combine mothering and work, therefore, may depend on the type of work you do, and for whom.

Working Mothers through History

So what are we to do? Devote our lives to fulfilling careers at the expense of harmonious relationships with our children? Give up our jobs to be perfect mothers and raise perfect children?

Women who choose the latter course sometimes think they're assuming a traditional role. But the truth is that mothers have always worked. In hunting, foraging, and agricultural societies, women's work—and not just nurturing—has through the millennia been indispensable to the survival of their families and communities. In most of the world today, this remains true. Outside of the highly industrialized countries, 90 percent of women must work for their and their families' living. Forty percent of the world's farmers are women. Where are their children while they work? Their babies ride on their backs or nestle against their bosoms in slings, while their older children toddle nearby or help out as best they can. A mother pauses in her work to nurse, and then returns to it while her child plays beside her or naps against her body, lulled by her motions. Or a grandmother or other relative watches over a group of children as their mothers work. As the children grow, they pitch in, having seen the work that must be done and how it must be done. Irenäus Eibl-Eibesfeldt, an ethologist who has studied tribal societies across the globe, points out that in most of them women spend at least 40 hours a week working—and working hard. These mothers would be most surprised to hear that being economically productive and being the mother of small children should be mutually exclusive.

In the West, too, through most of history, it would have been inconceivable for the great majority of women not to combine child care with work. Women's gardens, looms, and livestock formed the basis of cottage industry until the middle of the nineteenth century. A fascinating account of laboring women (in both senses of the word) is found in *The Midwife's Tale: The Life of Martha Ballard, Based on Her Diary 1785–1812*, by Laurel Thatcher Ulrich. Martha Ballard was a mother of nine and the midwife for 816 babies of other women who lived in and around Hallowell, Maine. Her diary documents how Early American women, like women before them, made their livings as they raised their children. Martha and other women in her community kept their own accounting books, documenting their trade in goods and services. Medicine, textiles, and garden produce were "strands of a broad and largely invisible local economy managed by women," writes Ulrich. These women, cultivating and preserving so that one harvest season stretched almost to the next, certainly worked as hard as we do. Their work, however, unlike that of many women today, did not require them to be separated from their children or to submerge their identities as mothers. Traditional women's work blended well with the raising of children.

The Industrial Revolution at first changed only the location of women's work. When industry moved from the cottage to the factory, both women and children moved along with it. This change in venue was disastrous for children, of course, who worked in exhausting, often dangerous jobs until child-labor laws were enacted in the early twentieth century. Eventually most factories became the province of a male work force, while most women remained at home, raising children, gardening, cooking, and sewing. These domestic crafts, however, gradually lost their economic necessity and clout; they were and are relegated to the trivial status of hobbies. During World War II most American women took jobs, to replace the men who had enlisted, but the women were ousted at the end of the war to make way for returning soldiers. It was then, in the late 1940s and 1950s, that the exclusive role of women as wives and mothers became a cultural ideal.

Of course, retiring to raise children was and is possible only for women whose husbands earn enough money to support a family. In poorer and single-parent families, women have never had the choice to be full-time at-home mothers. These women have always blended work and family, apologizing for neither, providing for both as best they can.

The period in which mothers were supposed to be economically unproductive to dedicate themselves to full-time child care and housework was but a brief blip in Western history. Today that period is over;

more than 50 percent of U.S. mothers of children under one year of age work outside their homes. In fact, the image of the "traditional family"—a working father, a homemaking mother, and one or more children—now represents only 9 percent of U.S. households. Nevertheless, the full-time homemaker lives on as a cultural ideal, spreading guilt among women who cannot live up to both her image and that of the career woman.

Mothers are working again. What's new is that we must be separated from our children while we work. And when we enter traditionally male fields, not only are we physically separated for most of each day, but we find we must be emotionally separated from our children as well.

What's Next?

Families today are reeling from the effects of these fundamental shifts in the structure of our lives. After all, as a species we have spent one hundred thousand years evolving physically, socially, and instinctually. In the tiniest final fraction in the time line of our existence, we've rearranged nearly all our social structures and forgotten most of our well-honed instinctual knowledge. We attempt even to fight our physical evolution as we go to extremes in exercising and dieting, and hold up bizarre physical attributes as cultural standards of beauty. We are rethinking, reshaping who we are as human beings. We've thrown the entire deck of cards into the air and they are raining down in disarray upon the heads of parents and children, who together make up the single social unit that has remained a constant since the beginning of human existence.

How then do we pick ourselves up, dust off the cultural flotsam and jetsam, and find the methods both new and old that are truly helpful to us as we give birth to babies, raise children, and perform useful, satisfying work? This book is an exploration of a few methods of combining work and parenting that have worked for others now and in the past—beginning with breastfeeding, the most time-honored, efficient, successful method of nurturing our babies while getting on with our lives.

CHAPTER TWO

WHY BREASTFEEDING IS IMPORTANT FOR YOU AND YOUR BABY

"Does it really matter whether I breastfeed my baby or not?"

THE DEBATE MAY NEVER end. Is breastfeeding best? Does it really make a difference whether a baby is breast- or bottle-fed? Although there are many reasons to choose to breastfeed your baby, perhaps the most compelling is that breast milk is filled with elements that provide optimum nourishment for your baby and protect her health in dozens of ways, now and far into the future. These elements cannot all be replicated by formula manufacturers.

In the past, scientists assumed that the reason breastfed babies had fewer infections than formula-fed babies was that breastfeeding allows less opportunity for contamination than bottle feeding does. Whereas milk taken directly from the breast has no chance to be contaminated, formula, which is mixed with water, put in a bottle, drunk through an artificial nipple, and perhaps left out and drunk again later has repeated opportunities to grow bacteria. But even infants fed rigorously sterilized formula have higher rates of meningitis, diarrhea, and ear, respiratory, and urinary tract infections than breastfed babies do. Scientists searched for another explanation of why bottle-fed babies tend to be so sickly.

Laboratory investigations have since produced volumes of proof that breast milk defends babies against infection, besides having myriad other health benefits. Many of the scientists doing the investigations, in fact, have turned into dedicated lactophiles with an abiding fascination for human milk. With every new discovery, their respect for the elegant efficiency of nature's system for nurturing babies grows. And working mothers who pump their breast milk on their lunch hours in borrowed offices and parked cars are doing so because they, too, understand that their own milk has no equal and no substitute.

The Immunologic Benefits of Breast Milk

All mammals feed their babies with milk. But just as a mouse differs from a whale, a cat from a kangaroo, and a woman from a cow, each species' milk is vastly different from that of other species. Horses and cows produce milk that grows bone and muscle quickly for babies that must be able to stand, walk, and run from the day of their birth. The very high-fat milk of a whale enables its baby to double its size in a few weeks and to withstand the cold seas. The milk of primates, including humans, promotes the rapid growth of brain tissue.

Infant mammals can survive on the milk of other species. Pigs have nursed kittens, and cats have nursed piglets. But young mammals fed this way miss out on the milk that is uniquely and perfectly designed for their optimal growth and development. As Karen Pryor points out in *Nursing Your Baby,* "This is especially true if the species are very different," as are humans and cows.

> *"The problems are great when you must modify the milk of hooved animals for infant human beings—if you wanted a really good match for us, you'd have to milk gorillas."*
>
> —KAREN PRYOR

So what is our own, perfectly tailored breast milk made of? To begin with, human milk is alive; fresh from the breast, it contains one million living cells per milliliter (or about one-third of a teaspoon). Colostrum, the honey-colored fluid that nourishes your baby for the first few days of life, contains up to seven million living cells per milliliter. Your placenta and blood nourished and protected your baby before birth, and your breasts, colostrum, and breast milk are designed to carry on the same vital functions after birth.

Most of the living cells in human milk are white cells similar to those in our blood. White cells search out and attack foreign bacteria on the surface of the baby's digestive organs and in the baby's tissues. Colostrum, the first milk, is full of white blood cells, so right from the beginning your newborn is protected against Coxsackie B virus and the bacteria *Salmonella,* streptococci, pneumococci, and the particularly nasty *E. (Escherichia) coli.* Every swallow your baby takes of colostrum or breast milk contains a tiny army of leukocytes and macrophages that surrounds and destroys the germs in its path. Although peak production of these protective cells occurs right after birth, they continue to be produced in effective quantities throughout the first year of nursing. In fact, levels of lysozyme, an enzyme produced by white cells that dissolves the cell walls of pathogens and is present in breast milk in quantities five thousand times higher than in cow's milk, actually increase for six months after birth and remain high through at least the second year of lactation. Some scientists believe that some of the white cells in milk also work to protect the breasts from infection in the first five to six weeks of lactation.

Thanks to this battalion of anti-infective cells, human milk is a far more stable substance than pasteurized cow's milk or formula. If a container of breast milk is left open in a warm room for several hours, it is likely to have a *lower* bacteria count hours later than it did at first. The protective forces in milk will have spent those hours scouring the milk for pathogens and destroying them. The white cells in breast milk can even survive freezing if the milk has been properly stored, and they proceed with their work when it is thawed. But they cannot survive heating, including microwaving and pasteurization. And they cannot be created artificially.

Human breast milk is also teeming with protective immunoglobulins. There are five basic types of immunoglobulins, and all are present in human milk. The most abundant type is known as secretory IgA. Produced in your breasts, IgA molecules bind themselves to pathogens that may find their way into your baby's stomach and intestines, and thereby prevent them from entering the tissues lining the gastrointestinal tract. In the early months, your baby's intestines are highly permeable, allowing foreign molecules and proteins to pass through and into your baby's blood, causing infection and allergies. IgA coats these vulnerable surfaces, forming a protective shield. Babies begin to produce secretory IgA on their own six to nine months after birth, but until then breast milk is their only source of this extraordinary protection.

Secretory IgA also enhances the effectiveness of the antibodies your body produces and passes through your milk to your baby. Your collection of antibodies matches the pathogens found in your and your nursing baby's environment. Whenever you ingest, inhale, or otherwise come in contact with a pathogen, your immune system manufactures an antibody designed to fight that specific germ. The constellation of antibodies that you pass on to your baby through your milk protect her from those same pathogens, the ones that your baby is most likely to encounter. Unfortunately, antibodies cause inflammation as they surround and attack disease-causing organisms, and inflammation can scar delicate lung and intestinal tissues. Secretory IgA molecules smooth the process, enabling antibodies to ward off infection without causing damaging inflammation.

Yet more elements in breast milk add to the arsenal of anti-infectives that keep your baby safe. The Bifidus factor promotes the growth of a beneficial organism, *Lactobacillus bifidus,* that crowds out harmful organisms. This benign intestinal flora is the reason breastfed babies' stools lack the strong smell of formula-fed babies'. Lactoferrin, a protein not found in cow's milk, limits the growth of bacteria, especially *Staphylococcus aureus,* by binding to the iron they thrive on and disrupting their digestion of carbohydrates. Similarly, the B_{12} binding protein inhibits the spread of bacteria by depriving them of the vitamin B_{12}. Interferon, present in mature milk and teeming in colostrum, is a well-known antiviral agent. Fatty acids found in breast milk damage the membranes of certain viruses, including the one that causes chicken pox, and may protect babies against intestinal parasites such as *Giardia lamblia* and *Entamoeba histolytica,* which causes amebic dysentery. Fibronectin, a protein in breast milk, enhances the ability of white cells to hunt for pathogens. This protein also helps to minimize inflammation; indeed, fibronectin may actually help repair tissue that has been damaged by inflammation. According to recent studies, numerous hormones and proteins in colostrum and breast milk cause the immune systems of breastfed babies to mature sooner than those of formula-fed babies. Probably for this reason, breastfed babies produce higher levels of antibodies in response to immunizations than do formula-fed babies.

Scientists continue to be intrigued by the powers of human breast milk, and to explore its significance to lifelong health. More discoveries are sure to come. Already clear, however, is that breast milk provides babies with far more than nutrients. In diverse and remarkable ways, breastfeeding protects your baby until her own immune system begins to function independently.

The Nutritive Value of Breast Milk

Of course, the fundamental purpose of breast milk is to nourish your baby—and the ways in which it does so are just as impressive as the ways in which it protects your baby from disease. Human milk consists of a solution of protein, sugar, and salts in which a variety of fatty compounds are suspended. It provides all the necessary nutrients and fluid for babies from birth to six months of age, and guarantees that older babies have a constant, easily digestible source of essential vitamins, protein, carbohydrates, cholesterol, and trace elements while they are beginning to eat solid foods.

Unlike formula out of a can, mother's milk varies from one woman to another, from one week to the next, and even from hour to hour through the day. Its changes seem to correspond to your baby's changing appetite and nutritional needs as he grows. The milk produced by mothers of premature babies, for example, is much higher in protein than that of mothers of full-term babies.

Fat provides 40 to 50 percent of the calories in breast milk. Despite many adults' dedicated avoidance of it, fat is essential for babies; it provides the energy they need to accomplish their astonishing growth rate. The fat in breast milk includes triglycerides, which are especially easy to digest, and prostaglandins. Although their function is not fully understood, prostaglandins may affect many physiologic processes, including circulation, gastric and mucous secretion, electrolyte balance, and zinc absorption.

The amount of fat in human milk varies according to several factors. Milk gets creamier over the course of a feeding, so the milk a baby gets at the end of the feeding is richest in fat. Also, the fat content of human milk goes up and down throughout the day, and is generally highest in the midmorning or early afternoon. Working mothers who pump their milk at these times provide their babies with especially hearty meals for the following day.

Babies also need cholesterol, and breast milk provides it as well. In fact, although cholesterol levels in human milk are quite high, they are low in cow's milk, and cholesterol is present in only trace quantities in formula. Cholesterol is required by your baby's rapidly growing nervous system, and it may also affect his intelligence, researchers believe. When children who were bottle-fed as premature babies were given IQ tests eight years later, those who had been fed breast milk scored an average of 8.3 points higher than did those who had received formula. Researchers also suggest that a naturally high-cholesterol diet in infancy fosters the mechanisms that will control cholesterol levels in later life.

The principal sugar in human milk is lactose, and it is present in far greater quantity in human milk than in other animal milks. Human milk contains 20 to 30 percent more lactose than cow's milk does, which is why human milk tastes so much sweeter. Lactose promotes the growth of beneficial bacteria in your baby's intestines, inhibits the growth of harmful bacteria, and enhances numerous other protective functions. Lactose enhances calcium absorption, so important to your baby's growing bones, and breaks down to produce galactose, an essential nutrient for the development of brain tissue. In fact, researchers have observed that among all mammals, the more lactose found in the milk, the larger the brain of the species. Since human milk contains so much more lactose than do formulas derived from cow's milk, the myriad benefits of lactose are more available to the breastfed than the bottle-fed infant.

Different animals grow at different rates, and these rates are apparently related to the level of protein in each species' milk. Humans grow slower than any other mammals, and human milk contains the least protein. Calves grow quite quickly, and cow's milk (and formula derived from it) is high in protein. The major proteins found in human and cow's milk are casein and whey, but whereas cow's milk contains 80 percent casein and 20 percent whey, whey predominates in human milk. With its low casein content, human milk forms small, soft, almost liquid curds that are easily digested, supplying a continuous flow of nutrients to the baby. In contrast, cow's milk, with its high casein content, forms a tough, rubbery curd that requires a high expenditure of energy for an incomplete digestion. The outdated recommendation that all babies, breast- or bottle-fed, be fed at four-hour intervals, seems to be based on the amount of time it takes a baby to digest these large, cow's milk curds. The idea that a baby will sleep longer if given a bottle of formula also stems from this longer, more difficult, and less effective digestive process. The stomach of the breastfed baby empties rapidly and easily (while the baby absorbs nearly all the nutrients provided by the milk). Consequently, the baby wants to nurse more often, generally every hour and a half to three hours during the daytime (and sometimes at night), for the first two to three months after birth. This in turn stimulates your milk production and establishes your milk supply.

The human infant uses the protein in breast milk with nearly 100 percent efficiency. Virtually all the protein in breast milk becomes part of the baby; little or none is excreted. The baby fed on cow's milk-based or vegetable-based formula, however, may waste about half the protein in his diet. Some of the protein passes undigested through his system and is excreted in the feces. Some is digested, but cannot be utilized by the cells of the body and is excreted in the urine. To get enough usable protein, the bottle-fed baby must drink a much larger volume of liquid than the breastfed baby. A working mother who knows this isn't concerned when her baby drinks one 8-ounce bottle of pumped breast milk at day care for another baby's two or three bottles of formula.

Cystine and taurine are other proteins not found in formula but abundant in human milk. Cystine is essential to skeletal growth, and taurine is needed for early brain development and maturation. Although the blood of breastfed infants is rich in cystine and taurine, that of infants fed formula contains very little of these essential proteins.

One of the most striking differences between human and cow's milk lies in its mineral composition. This difference, like that in protein levels, may be related to the rate of growth of the species for which the milk was intended. Human milk contains less than a quarter as much calcium as cow's milk; this appears to be all the calcium a full-term baby needs. Babies on cow's milk–based diets grow larger and heavier skeletons than breastfed babies in the first year of life. Iron, needed to make red blood cells, was once thought to be absent from breast milk. Now known to be present in low levels, the iron in breast milk has a high "bioavailability"; nearly 50 percent of it is absorbed by the baby's body. In contrast, only 10 percent of iron in plain cow's milk and 4 percent of iron in iron-fortified infant formulas is absorbed; the rest is digested or excreted through the kidneys.

There are other micronutrients in human milk, but their roles are not yet completely understood. Until a baby's need for a trace element is proven, formula manufacturers do not add it to their mixes. Infant formula, therefore, may lack many important micronutrients. Breast milk provides your baby with all necessary nutrients, whether or not scientists understand their significance.

Another significant difference between breastfeeding and formula feeding is that breastfeeding provides absolutely fresh milk, with all its vitamins still present. In the manufacture, storage, and reheating, some vitamins are inevitably lost.

As long as a breastfeeding mother eats a variety of nourishing foods and gets 15 minutes of sunshine on most days, she can be assured that her milk will satisfy the vitamin and mineral requirements of a full-term, healthy baby. Even when the mother's diet is not ideal, breast milk supplies all the nutrients babies need for their first five to six months. And breast milk continues to be a good source of nutrients later, as babies begin to eat solid foods. Mothers who breastfeed into the second and third year take comfort that their toddlers, so often picky eaters, are still receiving the spectrum of nutrients they need with each nursing.

Breast Milk and Allergies

Food allergies are believed to begin when foreign molecules penetrate the walls of a baby's intestinal tract and enter the bloodstream, causing mild to life-threatening reactions. Because the breastfed baby has received the benefit of secretory IgA and other elements that soothe and seal his intestinal surfaces, the baby can digest foreign proteins and molecules instead of absorbing them into his bloodstream. The formula-fed infant, however, may absorb whole proteins, and develop allergic reactions to them, well into her second year.

Allergic reactions are far less common in breastfed than in formula-fed babies. Cow's milk, eggs, chocolate, or citrus fruit in a mother's diet occasionally causes colic, or severe crying spells, in her breastfed baby, and if the mother drinks more than a few cups of coffee in a day, her baby may get jittery. But most of these reactions are symptoms not of true allergy but of a sensitivity to a substance in a food. Babies usually outgrow such sensitivities; in the meantime, their distress is quickly relieved when the mother stops eating the offending food. Formula-fed babies experiencing allergic reactions to the proteins in cow's milk or soy formula may not find relief so easily. Many are allergic to all but the very expensive hypoallergenic, or "predigested," formulas.

By six months of age, when nature intends a baby to sample new foods, food allergies are much less likely to become established. At this point many working mothers put away their pumps and allow their babies to be given formula or solids during their separations. Babies born into families with allergies, however, tend to begin producing secretory IgA later than do babies from families without this genetic inheritance. So if you have a family history of food allergies, you may want to delay the introduction of foods other than breast milk, especially those to which family members are allergic.

How do the immunologic and nutritive properties of human milk actually affect a baby's health? As study after study shows, exclusively breastfed babies have lower rates of diarrhea, vomiting, gastrointestinal infections, respiratory infections, and eczema than formula-fed babies do. Breastfed baby boys are less likely to have undescended testicles requiring surgical repair. Breastfed babies have less chance of succumbing to Sudden Infant Death Syndrome (SIDS). In the United States, in fact, formula-fed babies are hospitalized at a rate of up to 25 times higher than breastfed infants.

Breast milk's benefits continue long after weaning. As numerous studies have shown, babies fed breast milk tend to develop into children more intelligent than their formula-fed peers. Babies who are exclusively breastfed for at least six months, likewise, have less chance of developing childhood cancer, juvenile rheumatoid arthritis, or juvenile diabetes. They also appear less likely to develop multiple sclerosis, Crohn's disease, heart disease, and cancer later in life. A 1994 study in *Epidemiology* reported this largely unheralded fact: Women who were breastfed as babies, even if only for a short time, have a more than 25 percent lower risk of developing either premenopausal or postmenopausal breast cancer than do women who were formula-fed as babies. In general, scientists have found that the protection afforded by breast milk is greatest when formula feeding is excluded; this protection declines in proportion to the degree of supplementation with formula.

The Benefits of Breastfeeding for Mothers

Does breastfeeding have any benefits for you, the mother, besides the pleasures of having a healthy, happy baby? Would nature have designed it otherwise? Breastfeeding affords an astonishing array of maternal benefits, both physical and emotional, and short- and long-term.

During and after birth, your body produces the hormone oxytocin to initiate the let-down of your milk. Oxytocin simultaneously stimulates your uterus to contract; the contractions help to control blood loss and to return your uterus to its size before pregnancy. The hormone prolactin, secreted when your nipples are stimulated, suppresses ovulation as long as you nurse your baby frequently. In countries where babies are customarily nursed two to four years, breastfeeding functions as an essential birth-control method, guaranteeing that every baby receives sufficient nutrients and protection against disease before the next baby is born, and that the mother is not overtaxed by too-frequent childbearing.

Breastfeeding reduces a woman's risk of breast cancer. As a 1994 article in the *New England Journal of Medicine* states, "If women who do not breastfeed or who breastfeed for less than three months were to do so for four to twelve months, breast cancer among parous premenopausal women [women of childbearing age who have given birth at least once] could be reduced by eleven percent; if all women with children lactated for twenty-four months or longer, the incidence might be reduced by nearly twenty-five percent." Although research has turned up a host of factors that influence a woman's chance of getting cancer, breastfeeding is clearly one of the most significant. In populations where breastfeeding is the norm, the incidence of breast cancer is minimal. Among the Tanka of South China, who traditionally nurse their babies with their right breasts only, 80 percent of the breast cancer that develops in older women occurs in their left breasts, on which their babies never nursed. The exact mechanism by which breastfeeding thwarts cancer is unknown. It seems clear, however, that when our breasts are allowed to function as they are meant to they are healthier and stay healthier.

Breastfeeding has been found to protect against other diseases, too, including uterine, cervical, and ovarian cancers. Some researchers think breastfeeding protects against endometrial cancer, although more investigations must be done on this matter. Diabetic women who breastfeed have decreased insulin requirements while they're nursing, and women who breastfeed are one-fourth as likely to get osteoporosis as are women who formula-feed their babies. Women who breastfeed also tend to have fewer urinary tract infections.

Breastfeeding burns calories—more than 600 per day for women who don't give formula supplements. In one study, mothers who breastfed exclusively or partially had lost more fat around their hips and were closer to their prepregnant weights at three months postpartum than mothers who fed only formula.

And, as nursing mothers will tell you in chorus, breastfeeding has the most marvelous calming effect on them. A recent study documents their experience: At one month postpartum, breastfeeding women were significantly less anxious than formula-feeding women. The breastfeeding hormones, oxytocin and prolactin, cause a feeling of well-being that tends to promote maternal behavior. Also, the act of breastfeeding requires a woman to relax. No matter how hectic her life, a breastfeeding mother must sit or lie down with her baby eight or more times a day. And we mustn't discount the simple joy and peace of mind that come with cuddling a secure, satisfied, comfortable baby.

Whether or not they care that nursing is good for their health, most nursing mothers would say that breastfeeding's primary benefit is convenience. Although breastfed babies nurse more frequently than do formula-fed babies, the non-nursing mother must dedicate a great deal of time to purchasing and mixing formula, cleaning bottles and nipples, and warming bottles. Unlike formula, breast milk is always ready, warm, and, as long as the baby continues to nurse frequently, plentiful. When the baby is hungry, the breastfeeding mother simply finds a comfortable place to sit or lie down with him. At night, whereas the formula-feeding parent must wake up and get out of bed to prepare a bottle, the breastfeeding mother can have her baby brought to her, or, if her baby is sharing her bed, nurse without ever fully waking up. A breastfed baby is also highly portable: There are no bottles to pack and carry; there is no need to find a place to mix formula and heat the bottle. A spare diaper in her purse, and the breastfeeding mother and her baby are on their way.

The Benefits of Breastfeeding for Working Mothers

Many women going back to work decide that the "added stress" of nursing is the last thing they need. As many working women can attest, however, their lives are made easier rather than harder by breastfeeding. One experienced mother finds that "breastfeeding is the easier part of being a working mother. It's much harder finding time to iron a shirt."

The immunologic properties of breast milk benefit working parents as much as their babies. Breastfed babies wake their parents less often at night with earaches and stuffy noses. Because breastfed babies are generally healthier, they also tend to be happier. They cry less, smile more, and are less wearying to care for after a long day at work.

The anti-infective properties of breast milk are a real boon when a baby is or will be in group day care. Babies in day care are exposed to more germs than are babies cared for at home. But when these babies are breastfed, they are protected against many serious bacterial and viral infections and secondary complications. And the lower incidence and severity of illness in breastfed babies reduces the time their parents must take off from work.

The flood of relaxation that comes with the let-down of milk is made to order for stressed-out working mothers. You may find that, after nursing your baby at the end of the day, you have trouble remembering what had so vexed you at work just a few hours earlier. Your slate is wiped clean, and you can more easily and calmly attend to your family and yourself for the rest of the evening. A pediatrician comments, "My greatest release after coming home is putting up my feet and nursing the baby. We both feel wonderful. It is my unwinding time."

For the typical nursing and working mother, the most important benefit of breastfeeding is that day after day it confirms that she is irreplaceable to her baby. Most women who decide to breastfeed do so for their babies' sakes. Only later do they discover that it's good for them, too. For working mothers, breastfeeding is a friend, a constant ally against the anxiety that comes from having to leave their babies in someone else's care for most of the day, and wondering if they are good-enough mothers. For your baby, after all, the babysitter may be very nice, but only Mama has a soft, sweet-smelling breast and warm, sweet-tasting milk. And when you pick up the baby and nurse at the end of a work day, you and she are immediately a couple again. There is no "getting to know you again" period for a working mother and her nursing baby.

A physician says, "Nursing has been a wonderful way to reconnect with my children while working. My daughter's favorite time to nurse is right after I get home at the end of the day. Even though she now goes all day without nursing, she gets a little frantic once I get home, and she really wants to nurse. I have found that nursing puts life into perspective. The sense of accomplishment, bonding, and well-being that I get from nursing makes me less anxious about having to leave her during the day."

A book editor concurs. "I like that it keeps me feeling connected to him all day long. I'm forced to take 'baby time' when I'm at work, and I can even go see him and share our bond in the middle of a work day if I want. It helps ease the transition for me to nurse him when I drop him off and when I pick him up. I also feel like I'm still mothering him even when I'm not with him, by continuing to provide pumped breast milk for him."

A social worker who formula-fed her first baby and breastfed her second speaks poignantly of the difference: "Since my mother-in-law took care of my first child eight to ten hours a day and since she could feed him just as well as I could, sometimes I felt as though he was more hers than mine. Since I had to be away from him 40 hours a week, breastfeeding could have tied us back together at the end of the day. Not breastfeeding my son is one of the greatest regrets of my life. My experience with him made me determined to have a different experience when my daughter was born."

Breastfeeding after returning to work is a way to tie the two halves of your life together. It will help you to make sense of yourself in the challenging new role as mother while continuing your pre-baby work life. Learning the job of motherhood is hard enough without the distractions of responsibilities outside the home, but when you're trying to maintain your identity as a working woman you have an intensified need for the lessons taught by breastfeeding. You can rely on breastfeeding as a blueprint for the intuitiveness, nurturing, and empathy that comes with experienced mothering. Through breastfeeding, you can give your child the best possible beginning, and in return you will gain confidence in yourself as a mother.

Parenting by Instinct

Once we consider all the aspects of breastfeeding—behavioral, immunologic, and nutritive—we cannot help but be impressed by how perfectly we humans have evolved to feed our babies. This may lead us to wonder what other special baby-care behaviors have evolved with our species. If you traveled now to societies that are still much the same as they have been for thousands of years, what would you see? How do parents take care of babies in cultures unchanged by such technological marvels as the clock, the baby bottle, and the baby carriage?

Ethologists, or researchers in the biologic bases of human behavior, have studied traditional cultures in every part of the world. They have identified a collection of ways in which parents all over the world care for their babies. These ways can be assumed to be humankind's basic parenting practices—practices that have evolved with our species. Like breast milk, they are perfectly matched to the needs of the human baby.

In every traditional society we know about, mothers keep their babies with them most of the time, from the moment of birth on. They breastfeed until their babies are ready to wean or until another baby is born or expected. They respond to their babies' cries quickly and without fear of "spoiling" them. They carry or "wear" their babies for most of each day, unless someone else in the family or tribe is carrying or playing with them. And, in every indigenous society, mothers sleep with their babies. These are the ways in which human beings have nurtured their babies since the beginning of time.

William Sears, a pediatrician, and his wife, Martha, a nurse, studied parenting styles among hundreds of families in southern California. They paid particular attention to those parents who seemed to enjoy raising children and whose children seemed to be turning out well. From their observations, the Searses developed a list of parenting practices that work well. Their list is composed of the very same five practices that researchers have observed among parents in so many traditional cultures.

The renowned naturalist Jane Goodall, for lack of a better role model in her jungle-based research station, decided to care for her baby as some of our closest cousins, the chimpanzees, do theirs. What did she do? She carried her baby with her wherever she went. She let him sleep in her bed. She responded quickly to his cues, as she had seen mother chimps do, and she breastfed him. As explains Jean Leidloff, who lived for several years with the Yequana Indians of South America and admired their gentle, skillful parenting (which consisted of the same five basic practices), "We have had exquisitely precise instincts, expert in every detail of child care, since long before we became anything resembling *Homo sapiens.*"

INSTINCTUAL PARENTING PRACTICES

- Breastfeeding without restriction
- Keeping the baby close from birth on
- Carrying or "wearing" the baby
- Responding quickly to the baby's cues
- Sleeping together

As modern "civilized" parents, we are deluged with new "proven" strategies for taking care of our babies, from bottle feeding on a schedule to letting them cry for hours so that they learn to fall asleep alone. We try out every new theory in hopes that it will ease this job of being a parent, the hardest we've ever known. Perhaps we are searching for answers because we have forgotten what we once knew so well. Perhaps being a parent is not supposed to be so hard.

Does this mean that, if you want to be the mother you were evolved to be, to care for your baby perfectly, you must sleep with her, carry her at all times, jump every time she peeps, and never be separated from her, beginning with the moment of birth? No, of course not. Mothers in traditional societies think of these practices not as rigid rules but just as what comes naturally *most* of the time. These mothers are simply doing what feels right. And, remember, they have many helping hands with both baby care and other kinds of work. A baby in these kin-based societies is passed around all day long from her mother to her father to her siblings to her cousin's husband's mother, showered with love as she goes. Few American mothers live in a harmonious, helpful extended family. But if you're hearing conflicting advice about the "right" way to care for your baby, it is useful to know what mothers knew before anyone thought to tell them anything at all.

This knowledge is especially useful when you are going back to work and wish to minimize the effect of each day's separation on your relationship with your baby. You can draw from this ancient pool of mothering knowledge to stay close to your baby. Think of these five practices—staying together, breastfeeding for a year or more, responding sensitively and quickly to your baby's cues, carrying or "wearing" your baby, and sharing your bed with your baby—as tools in your parenting toolbox. You may not use them all, but you may find one or two especially handy. If you and your baby were not able to be together for the first hours or even days after birth, or if letting your baby sleep in your bed is unappealing, it's okay. Human evolution has provided you with an array of ways to ensure that you and your baby stay closely bonded. And the fact that you, like mothers through time, will also be working each day need make no difference at all. When and how these instinctual parenting practices may be of use to you in staying close to your baby will be discussed in the following chapters.

CHAPTER 3

BREASTFEEDING BASICS

*"I never saw a baby nursing until I
nursed my own."*

LIKE MOTHERING IN GENERAL, breastfeeding is a learned
art requiring practice and, usually, help from women who have successfully breastfed their own babies. Ideally, learning to breastfeed
begins when you are breastfed yourself and continues as you grow up
watching mothers in your family and community nurse their babies.
Even chimpanzees who are raised in captivity without other chimps
around them must be shown how to hold their babies and how to nurse
them. In higher primates, including humans, the knowledge of how to
feed our infants relies more on experience and observation than on
instinct.

Most Western women who have grown up in the past fifty years
have only occasionally, if ever, seen babies put to the breast. In the
fifties, sixties, and early seventies, few women breastfed at all, and
although breastfeeding has regained popularity since then, many
women still refuse to nurse in public or even in front of family members. So young women and girls have been unable to learn the art of
breastfeeding as primates are designed to, by watching their elders. To

confound matters, women's magazines, toy stores, and television are full of bottle-feeding images. A nursing mother was taken aback when her toddler "who had never had a bottle in his mouth" suggested that a visitor's fussy baby might feel better if he were given a bottle. Culture is a pervasive thing; it sinks into our thoughts deeper and earlier than we might assume.

If you have not grown up watching nursing mothers, if you were not breastfed yourself, or if you tried to nurse a previous baby and could not, take time now to learn all you can about nursing from experienced mothers and, if possible, a professional lactation consultant. You may wish to attend a La Leche League meeting in your community. An international organization of nursing mothers helping nursing mothers, La Leche League can be an invaluable source of accurate and empathetic breastfeeding advice. As a working mother, however, you may find some League leaders and meetings oriented to stay-at-home moms rather than mothers with jobs. If you don't feel comfortable in the first League meeting you attend, or if you find that the first leader you speak with on the phone seems unsupportive of working mothers, try another group or another leader, since each group has its own unique character. Unfortunately, La Leche League has acquired a reputation for hostility toward working mothers who rely on substitute caregivers. In fact, only a minority of La Leche members are dogmatically opposed to maternal employment. League leaders are dedicated to helping all mothers, whether they are going back to work or not, and are glad to provide the one-on-one breastfeeding assistance that can make all the difference in the world. You can reach a La Leche League leader by telephone or through the Internet (see "Resources," page 165).

Several excellent general books on breastfeeding are listed in "Resources." Although this book will give you all the basics on getting a good start in breastfeeding, other books can tell you how to handle special situations. Attend a breastfeeding class while you are pregnant, if possible. Educate your mate along with yourself; his support and enthusiasm for breastfeeding may be the key to your success.

The Very Beginning

For the best start in breastfeeding, nurse as soon after birth as your baby is ready. Researchers believe that the first minutes after birth offer an optimal opportunity (although not the only one) for a mother and baby to establish a strong emotional attachment. Babies tend to be strikingly alert during the first hour after birth, a time when their parents are very eager to interact with them. Numerous studies have demonstrated the lasting benefit of this initial socializing. One study revealed that mothers who held their babies for the first hour after birth spoke more to their children even a full two years later than did mothers who were separated from their babies during the first hour. The mothers who had had the early contact asked twice as many questions of their children as the control group of mothers did, and gave fewer commands. Asking questions is a sign of a harmonious relationship; commands express aggressive dominance. Another study showed that mothers who socialized with their babies right after birth felt more competent and less anxious than mothers who were separated from their babies.

Babies display a readiness to suck during the first two hours after birth that is not as strong again until forty hours later. If you nurse soon after birth, your baby's sucking will help contract your uterus by stimulating release of the hormone oxytocin. Besides planting the seed for a powerful and lasting emotional attachment, your first contact with your baby can help ensure your physical health.

Although most hospitals no longer routinely separate mothers and babies after birth, you may still need to state your preferences on the matter. Let your doctor and the hospital staff know that you intend to nurse as soon as possible after giving birth, whether in the delivery room after a vaginal birth or in the recovery room after a cesarean section.

While you're in the hospital, plan on "rooming in," or keeping your baby in your room with you rather than in the nursery. Ask the hospital staff in advance whether you will need a private room if you're to keep your baby with you both day and night. In their book *A Good Birth, A Safe Birth,* Diana Korte and Roberta Scaer recommend that you "be specific. Describe what you want. Don't ask if you can have your baby with you as much as you want. You might get a clearer answer if you ask instead what hours of the day you cannot have your baby. Then, they may reply that you can have your baby whenever you want, except during visiting hours (three hours in the afternoon and another three hours in the evening); at night . . . ; and for an hour in the morning when the pediatricians come in to check the babies in the nursery." You may need to be clear that when you say you want your baby with you at *all* times, you mean it. If the hospital does not seem agreeable, you may want to investigate any other hospitals or birthing centers that may be available to you. Or have your doctor write on your chart an order for full-time rooming-in.

Contrary to what many people believe, mothers who keep their babies with them 24 hours a day become no more fatigued than do mothers whose babies stay in the nursery. After all, you can doze and nurse at the same time, as you could never do while holding a bottle. Rooming-in allows you to feed your baby whenever and for however long both you and he wish, day and night, which is the very best way to guarantee a bountiful milk supply in the days to come. He will cry much less with you than he would in the nursery, too.

Keeping your baby with you means that you will know him better and feel more confident caring for him when the time comes to leave the hospital. You'll be less likely to experience the astonished panic so many parents recall on discharge. Establishing your trust in yourself as a competent mother will be the greatest gift you can give yourself, your baby, and your family in the days ahead.

> *"Wait, are they going to let me just walk off with him? I don't know beans about babies!"*
>
> —ANNE TYLER

If for medical reasons you and your baby must be separated after birth, don't despair. Developing a deep bond between any two people always takes time, and learning to become a mother does not happen all at once. (Experienced mothers say this is a lifelong process!) You have much time ahead of you to get to know and love your baby. Breastfeeding, carrying your baby, and sleeping with him will be especially helpful for the two of you.

Getting Started

Your nurse or midwife will help you put your baby to the breast for the first time. To begin, you will need to know a few basic facts about breastfeeding.

Proper positioning of your baby at the breast is the most important way to prevent or reduce nipple soreness, stimulate your milk production, and ensure a good milk supply for weeks or months to come. Hold your baby so that her tummy and knees are against your tummy, and her head is nestled in the bend of your elbow. Or use the crossover hold: Hold the baby with the arm opposite from the breast you're starting with, support her neck and head with your hand, and position her face directly in front of your breast. Use pillows wherever you need them to prop up your baby, your arm, or both. Your baby should not have to turn her head to reach your nipple with her mouth—and you should not have to lean over to reach her mouth with your nipple.

Proper positioning is essential to successful breastfeeding. Hold your baby so that her tummy and knees are against your tummy, and her head is nestled in the bend of your elbow.

Holding your baby so that she must turn her head to reach your nipple, or so that you must lean over, will cause sore nipples and other breastfeeding difficulties.

Next, let your baby latch on to your nipple only when her mouth opens *very* wide, as if she were yawning. Squeeze a few drops of colostrum onto her lips, or tickle her lips with your nipple to get her interested. As soon as she opens wide, pull her close so that the tip of her nose barely touches your breast. Don't lean over her, but bring her to you. Press her firmly to your breast; babies' noses, turned up and slightly flared, are able to breathe even when pressed against a breast. Cup your breast with your free hand to support it.

If your baby is sucking just the nipple rather than as much of your areola as her mouth can hold, she is not latched on properly. Take her off and try again. Remember, you are both learning this dance together. As your baby nurses, your nipple should be drawn to the rear of her throat and her gums should be around your areola. You know your baby is properly latched on when she has taken in an inch or more of the lower areola in her mouth (this may be all of the lower areola or just part of it) and when her chin and the tip of her nose are touching your breast. Check to see that your baby's lips are relaxed outward, like fish lips, rather than pulled in.

Before taking your baby off the breast, watch for cues that she has finished. Generally, a baby will let go of the breast on her own, and often she'll fall asleep. When you switch her to the other side, she may awaken to suck some more.

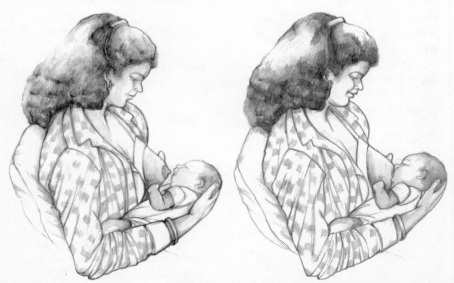

When your baby opens her mouth very wide, as if yawning, pull her directly onto the nipple.

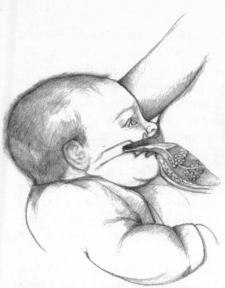

As your baby nurses, your nipple should be drawn to the rear of her throat and her gums should be around your areola.

If your baby is sucking on just the nipple, and not the areola as well, take her off the breast and try again.

If you do wish to take your baby off the breast before she lets go on her own, break the suction between her mouth and your nipple by slipping your finger into the corner of her mouth. Pulling a baby off without breaking the suction first can stretch the nipple and make it sore.

Even if you can't feel your milk letting down, you can tell when it does by watching your baby's sucking rate. Her quick, short sucks will change to a steady pattern of one or two sucks followed by a swallow, and a little wiggle at her ears and temples. (At least six wet cloth diapers and two to five bowel movements a day, after the third day, will confirm that your baby is latching on and sucking well. If you use very absorbent disposables, expect them to feel heavy rather than wet. Three to four heavy disposables are equivalent to six to eight wet cloth diapers.)

Put out the number of diapers you expect to use first thing in the morning. If you go through them all by the next morning, you will know that your baby is getting enough milk.

Hospital nurses and pediatricians sometimes recommend that you limit the first nursings to 5 minutes on each breast, then gradually increase the time to 10 and 15 minutes. This is supposed to prevent sore nipples, but it doesn't. Besides, most newborns need to suck for 5 minutes just to get the milk. If your baby is positioned and latched on well, there is no need to watch the clock.

After the first few feedings, try nursing in other positions—lying down or with your baby turned so that her feet face the opposite direction. With frequent nursings (every two hours or less), you will find after a few weeks that you hardly have to think about positioning and latch-on at all; both you and your baby will settle into a correct position naturally and comfortably whether you are sitting up or lying down—or, as time goes by, talking on the phone or working at the computer.

Once you've finished your first nursing, you've passed your first lesson in sensitive mothering. From this moment forward, your baby's cues, and your growing child's cues, are your best guide to your own actions as her mother. Watch your baby, not the clock. Listen to your own feelings, not your neighbor's or your mother-in-law's. Breastfeeding will teach you to read your baby's subtle, unspoken language. The sensitivity you thus acquire will be the foundation of a deep attachment and harmonious relationship between mother and child—a relationship that cannot be disrupted even by daily separations when you return to work.

Preventing Engorgement

Your milk will come in gradually, beginning, probably, on the second or third day after birth. When you feel your breasts getting fuller you should nurse frequently, even if you have to wake the baby to do so. This will minimize engorgement, which occurs when the breasts fill with milk until they become larger and firmer, in some cases astonishingly big and hard. Your breasts are not intended to store milk, but they will hold some, if it is not withdrawn, while you become increasingly uncomfortable. Engorgement can also make latching on a challenge for your baby. Frequent nursings right from the beginning will turn your colostrum to mature milk quickly, reduce engorgement, and make it easier for your baby to latch on to your nipples.

Avoiding Sore Nipples

Breastfeeding is not supposed to hurt. Nevertheless, sore nipples are so common that they are sometimes considered inevitable. Nipple pain is usually most intense the moment the baby latches on, and lessens as the milk lets down. The tenderness soon disappears altogether if the baby is positioned and sucking well.

If your nipples begin to get sore, allow them to air-dry between nursings, and avoid wearing a bra (especially while sleeping). Don't limit your baby's nursing time; frequently putting the baby on and taking him off the breast may aggravate the problem, besides upsetting the baby.

For advice on healing sore and cracked nipples, see page 52.

Seeking Help

If your nipples become exceedingly sore or if your baby has difficulty latching on and staying on the breast, seek the help of a professional lactation consultant. Do this *before* you leave the hospital, if possible. Many maternity wards now have a lactation consultant; the nurses will ask her to stop by your room if you request it. You may be able to visit a breastfeeding clinic, or even hire a lactation consultant to visit you at home. Or you can consult with a La Leche leader. Early observation and guidance by an expert can keep most breastfeeding problems from becoming serious. Beware of accepting casual advice from friends, relatives, or even pediatricians and nurses who haven't studied lactation or breastfed successfully themselves. "You may not be making enough milk," they may tell you. "Why don't you give the baby a bottle, just this time?" Careful observation will reveal the cause of whatever problem you are having (not having enough milk is one of the *least* likely), and an experienced person can help you find its solution.

How Your Breasts Produce Milk

If you are planning to go back to your job within a few weeks or months, you may be wondering how being away from your baby for hours each day will affect breastfeeding. Understanding how and when your breasts produce milk will enable you to manage your milk supply and meet your baby's nutritional needs.

When your nipples are stimulated, your brain releases the hormones prolactin and oxytocin, which in turn cause your breasts to secrete and release milk. Prolactin is the milk-producing hormone. The more frequently and effectively your baby sucks, the more prolactin your body releases and the more milk your breasts produce. Oxytocin is the milk-ejection hormone. It contracts the sacs where milk is made to push the milk through ducts to the sinuses just behind the nipple. This sudden release of milk is your "let-down reflex." Your baby takes milk from your breast by sucking, but you are also *giving* milk by letting it down. Both actions are required for successful breastfeeding. In the early weeks of breastfeeding a vigorous let-down can eject milk with hilarious gusto, spraying it in twin fountains. When let-down occurs, the baby hardly needs to milk the breast; the milk is pumped

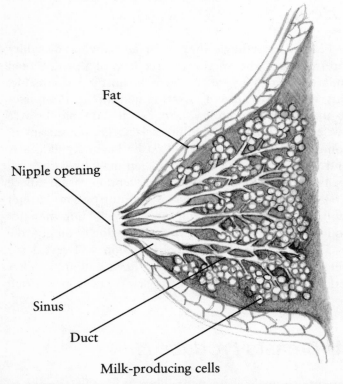

Milk is made in grape-like clusters of sacs in the back of the breast. The "let-down reflex" ejects milk from the sacs and delivers it to the sinuses behind the nipple.

into her throat. Your milk may let down several times in the course of a feeding.

Letting down your milk is crucial to your baby's nutrition. The milk that is stored in the sinuses and can be drawn out by sucking alone is low in fat. It may satisfy your baby's need for fluid and is perfect for times when your baby is only thirsty or just nursing for comfort. After the milk lets down, however, comes your baby's wonderfully satiating square meal—milk that is held in the cells farther back in your breast and gets creamier as the feeding progresses. Dr. F. E. Hytten, of the University of Aberdeen in Scotland, has demonstrated with the help of sponges that fat particles in breast milk tend to cling to the walls of the alveoli and ducts and to be drawn off last. The baby's last few swallows of milk from the first breast nursed contain the most fat of all (assuming a let-down has occurred and the baby comes off the breast only when she is ready). The fat mixes more evenly in the second breast, although some gradation remains. Dr. Michael Woolridge identified several English babies who were failing to gain weight because their mothers had been firmly told to nurse only 10 minutes on each breast at each feeding; following that rule, the mothers were feeding their babies on what was essentially skim milk.

A good breast pump stimulates let-down just as your baby does. Being able to let down your milk in response to the stimulation of your pump is essential if you are to collect significant amounts of milk after you return to work.

In the early months, your milk may let down anytime you are reminded of your baby. You might be talking to a friend on the phone, telling her about the baby, and suddenly feel the tingle of your milk letting down and a spreading dampness in your bra and blouse. The sound of your baby's cry may bring down your milk in a gush. When you begin pumping your milk at work, you may find that you can prompt your let-down reflex by looking at a picture of your baby as you pump or by breathing in the scent of a nightie your baby wore the night before. You may even associate the pump itself with your baby, and so find your milk letting down as soon as you get out the pump.

The let-down reflex can also be conditioned to certain times during the day. If your baby settles into a regular feeding pattern, his meal may be ready and dripping before you even put him to the breast. In the same way, when you begin pumping your milk at work, you may find your milk letting down as soon as you turn the lock in the door of the room in which you pump.

In time the system settles down; leaking and spraying may become a memory of newborn days. Until then, add a collection of cotton breast pads to your nursery supplies, and tuck a couple into your nursing bra each day.

Establishing Your Milk Supply

Breastfeeding is a supply-and-demand system; that is, your breasts produce milk in response to sucking. When there is more sucking (by a well-positioned baby or a good pump), they produce more milk; when there is less sucking, they make less milk. If ever you feel that your milk production is tapering off, simply increase the number of times you put your baby to the breast each day and, if necessary, pump your milk just after nursing or an hour or two after your baby begins a long sleep stretch. Frequent short nursings (20-minute sessions every two hours or so) will be more effective than longer but less frequent sessions.

> *The law of supply and demand: The more you nurse your baby (or pump your milk), the more milk your body will produce.*

As a working mother, you may notice fluctuations in your milk supply more than other mothers do. You may see your milk supply decrease over the course of the work week, build back up over the weekend, be quite plentiful on Monday, and then gradually decrease again as the week proceeds. Because you understand breastfeeding as a supply-and-demand system, you will know what to expect—and how to manage it. Specific techniques for managing your milk supply are described in Chapter 5.

Going Home

These days you are likely to be sent home from the hospital a day or two after your baby is born or, if you've had a cesarean section, on the third day. Your milk probably won't have come in yet. If your baby has been sleepy she may not have nursed very much yet. Sixty years ago, mothers and babies stayed in the hospital one to two weeks after delivery. Being sent home then meant that the mother and baby were deemed to have learned all the basics (of bottle-feeding, at least) and were ready to be on their own. But, these days, when a 24-hour-old mother is discharged with a 24-hour-old baby, it is not because they are necessarily well prepared to go home, but because insurance companies have found a dandy way to save a lot of money.

Of course many mothers are happy to leave the hospital as soon as possible, thereby avoiding the rules, schedules, routine separations from their babies, and supplementary feedings of glucose water that were once standard in every hospital and still are in many (not to mention the noise and bad food). But going home without the support you need there can be as challenging as avoiding hospital interventions.

In recent years, somehow, American mothers have grown fond of the myth of the pioneer woman who planted the fields in the morning, gave birth without assistance to a healthy baby at midday, and spent the rest of the afternoon baking bread. If those women could do it, the moral is, so can we, in our modern way: We can work up until the day before labor, go to the hospital and give birth, then come home and call work. A 1985 guide to pregnancy and birth for career women exalts the advertising executive who "felt so ready to go back to work that she met her housekeeper in the lobby of the hospital and let her take the baby home while [she] went back to the office."

In past centuries, societies had stringent rules and rituals for taking care of new mothers and babies; some societies still have such rules and rituals. These traditions have worked to keep the mother well rested and nourished and to strengthen the attachment that is—or at least was—so essential to the infant's survival. In Jamaica and many other places, the midwife stayed on for a few days after birth to look after any other children and to do the cooking or washing for the family, so that the mother could rest and focus on her new baby. In southern India, a mother stays with her newborn in a special hut for 90 days, visited only by her husband and midwife. Among the Hopi, a mother and baby remained in a darkened room for 18 days. The Lummi of the Northwest coast required a 12-day seclusion period for mother, baby, and father, all of whom are attended by the "helping women." In ancient Japan, both parents and their newborns were secluded for 35 days, and even today Japanese babies are rarely taken out of the home until they are a month old. In most societies, a new mother is still fed special foods to make her strong and her milk bountiful. "Thus the initial learning time in which mother and baby become attached to each other is safeguarded and given special ritual significance by the culture," writes Sheila Kitzinger, social anthropologist and author of numerous books on birth and motherhood. Women in traditional societies go back to work, of course, but only after their transition to motherhood is well begun.

There is no doubt a biological basis to these worldwide postpartum traditions. Prolactin, the milk-making hormone, is highest in a mother's bloodstream for the first 40 days after delivery. Prolactin levels then decline, though very gradually, as the mother continues breastfeeding. How then do many women continue nursing their babies for two years or more, past the point when prolactin disappears from their systems? What keeps up the milk-making process? One hypothesis is that the high levels of prolactin generated by exclusive breastfeeding in the first six weeks may somehow enable the breasts to work independently of the prolactin stimulus after this period. Perhaps ancient peoples understood that a generous confinement period helped a mother establish her milk supply. They may have noticed a better survival rate in infants who were secluded with their mothers.

Kittie Frantz, a widely respected pediatric nurse practitioner, put this hypothesis into practice in Santa Monica, California. Approximately 90 percent of her patients were working nursing mothers, and nearly all of them complained that they had difficulty maintaining their milk supplies when they went back to work. The common practice in the area was to begin pumping and feeding pumped milk to babies at two weeks of age to get them used to a bottle early on. Frantz began to recommend freezing the pumped milk and delaying bottle feeding until a baby was four to five weeks old. When her patients followed this advice, their success in maintaining bountiful milk supplies was, Frantz says, "phenomenal." These mothers would ask her, "Why do I have so much milk for my baby when all my friends are struggling?" Her answer: "We heeded the wisdom of the women who came before us."

Safeguard this time, the first six weeks or so after giving birth to your baby. It is your babymoon. Before the baby is born, preferably, ask your mother or your mother-in-law, a sister or a dear friend, to come and help out—not with the baby but with meals, housekeeping, and caring for your other children, if this is not your first baby. Ideally, this helper—or "doula," as such a person is often called—will also be experienced in breastfeeding, or at least supportive of it. The father, of course, may take this role, but it is the rare husband who can take more than a week off work to help out at home. Besides, a father should also have the opportunity to focus on his new child without the constant distraction of housework and cooking. Many grandmothers visit for a couple of weeks whenever a grandchild is born, to help the new mother so she can care for her new baby without distraction. One mother remembers her own mother's visit with a smile: "I never changed a diaper the first month. I never shopped or cooked or cleaned. I lived from feeding to feeding, every two hours."

Ideally, your helper should not plan to spend nights at your house. You'll need extra help, not extra bodies, in your home. One experienced grandmother, who usually stays with the family when she visits, takes a room at a nearby inn or sleeps at a friend's house when a baby is born. She helps her daughter through the day, then prepares dinner, kisses her son-in-law as he walks in after work, and departs, leaving the parents to baby-gaze in private for the evening. They much appreciate her sensitivity to the needs of the family as it adjusts to its newest incarnation.

Your mother or mother-in-law may or may not support your decision to breastfeed. A lack of breastfeeding support is a primary reason that many women give up nursing in the early days or weeks. Remember that when your mother or mother-in-law gave birth bottle-feeding was standard. She may feel uncomfortable or even guilty because she didn't nurse her babies. She may have been looking forward to sharing the feeding of a grandchild, and may now feel disappointed.

If this is the case in your family, finding breastfeeding support and assistance from an experienced friend, a La Leche League leader, or a lactation consultant will be all the more essential. Call La Leche League or the International Lactation Consultant Association (see "Resources") for a referral, or ask the nurses in your maternity ward for recommendations. Investigate postpartum support services in your area. Doulas-for-hire are now available in most major cities and their suburbs, and some provide lactation counseling as well as domestic help. Look in your local parents' paper, if there is one, for advertisements. You might consider hiring a postpartum service for the first three or four days after birth and asking a relative to come and help when you first return to work (see Chapter 6 for more on this subject).

Accept all offers of help from friends and neighbors. If you don't know what help you'll need, say you'll call them, or have your mate or doula call them, once you are home with the baby. Anne Lamott, a single mother, remembers one night not long after her baby was born, when a visitor from her church, a man in his sixties, arrived at the door. "After exchanging pleasantries he said, 'I wanted to do something for you and the baby. So what I want to ask is, What if a fairy appeared on your doorstep and said that he or she would do any favor for you at all, anything you wanted around the house that you felt too exhausted to do by yourself and too ashamed to ask anyone else to help you with?'

" 'I can't even say,' I said. 'It's too horrible.' But he finally convinced me to tell him, and I said it would be to clean the bathroom. He ended up spending an hour scrubbing the bathtub and toilet and sink with Ajax and lots of hot water. I sat on the couch while he worked, watching TV, feeling vaguely guilty and nursing Sam to sleep." Such kindly fairies are all too rare, for we are not meant to enter into parenthood alone and without help.

On discharge from the hospital, you will probably be given a good-bye gift of baby-care pamphlets, perhaps tucked into a basket with a pair of booties or a rattle, a few disposable diapers, and a can of baby formula. Take the booties and the diapers, but leave the can. Giving "formula kits" to all new mothers, including breastfeeding mothers, is a widespread hospital practice funded by formula manufacturers. The message is implicit that you need formula "just in case"—that breastfeeding is an experiment that may not work out. The formula manufacturers hope you will try out their product at some point in the early weeks—which is easy to do if it is sitting on your kitchen shelf—and thus begin the cycle of supplementation that so often leads to early weaning. But you won't face this temptation if you leave the bait behind.

Some mothers are surprised to find the trip home from the hospital exhausting. Be sure to go straight to bed, and tuck your baby in beside you. You need rest so you'll retrieve your strength, and to nurse frequently to help your milk come in, if it hasn't already. Provided you have plenty of tender care by people who love you, home is the best place to establish lactation.

CHAPTER FOUR

LIFE ON LEAVE: THE FOURTH TRIMESTER

"Breastfeeding lets me tell my baby things with my body that she wouldn't understand with words for a long time."

Becoming a Mother

When you give birth to a baby, you also give birth to a mother. Expect the weeks and (with luck) the months of your maternity leave to be an intense interval in your life. Not only are you learning to understand and to answer your baby's unique needs, but your sense of self is undergoing a tectonic shift.

If this is your first baby, your inner task at this time is to integrate your identity as a mother into your established identity. Women experience this process with varying degrees of ease and upheaval. If you have built your self-image largely on your work, and if you relish your independence, you may find this new identity especially hard to embrace. To compound the difficulty, your work may demand that you separate your personal life from your professional life (as men have always done). But, as psychologist Joyce Block writes, "motherhood is not an experience that is easily compartmentalized." As a mother, you are no longer a lone individual. Although the umbilical cord has been cut, you and your baby remain connected emotionally and, if you are breast-feeding, physically, for many months after birth. For your newborn, you are the world. He relies on you to anticipate his needs, to interpret his cries, and to protect and nurture him just as your womb has done for the preceding nine months. And you now see life through a new lens, a lens with your child's image indelibly etched on its surface.

Your emotional bond with your baby, already well begun, deepens by incalculable fathoms during these early months. This may be the most wonderful journey you've ever taken, and yet at times you may feel in over your head. Enter into this stage knowing that you will eventually emerge as yourself but with new, rich dimensions. Sometimes, during this period, your old life may seem distant and unrelated to your new state of existence. The tidal wave of changes may tower so high that you wish you could build a wall against it before you are overwhelmed and your life is forever altered beyond recognition. You may find yourself trying to prevent changes from occurring, or denying that they have occurred. Yes, you've had a baby, but other than that, you insist, everything is the same. The truth is that nothing is the same, nor will anything ever be quite the same again. Your task is now to build a new reality that incorporates your motherhood.

In many ways our culture encourages parents to ignore their instincts, which are thought to create bad habits. Just about everything a mother does because she wants to, because it seems like the easiest thing to do, and because it makes her baby happy—whether picking up a baby when he cries, or breastfeeding without a schedule, or bringing a baby into the parents' bed to sleep—has been labeled a bad habit by one expert or another. Shrug off these contrived ideas. When your baby cries and you feel the urge to go to him, to put him to your breast, to make right what he feels is wrong, remember that you are the expert on caring for your baby. The blood flow to your breast is increasing because your body knows what to do and is already responding, even if your mind has been convinced to hesitate.

Research confirms that your responsiveness to your baby's cues—whether crying, rooting, fussing, eye contact, or any other form of infant communication—is the most important contributor to your baby's physical, emotional, and intellectual development. Your quick responses tell your baby that his actions are meaningful, that he is a person whose needs matter. Your sensitive interactions guide and encourage his developing sense of self. Responding to your baby, picking him up and cuddling him when he cries, putting him to your breast and soothing him, teaches him trust. He trusts you to meet his needs. It is this basic trust that will form the core of his self-esteem as he grows.

Following your maternal instincts is as important to your development as it is to your baby's. Each interaction with your baby refines your mothering skills and enhances your understanding of your baby. Through caring for your baby, you will grow, too. If you attend to your baby's needs lovingly now, she is more likely to grow into someone who nurtures others readily and who is easy to be with. As Michael Schulman and Eva Mekler, psychologists and authors of *Bringing Up a Moral Child,* conclude of the results of one wide-scale study, "children who were treated with sensitivity and cooperation tend to be sensitive and cooperative in turn." When you are trying to keep work and family life in balance, you will want to spend the hours at home in positive interactions with your child rather than in struggles of will. Now is the time to establish a deep, immutable harmony.

Experienced mothers who enjoy mothering, whether employed or not, would urge you to open the floodgates. Wallow in your passion for your baby, and in hers for you. Holding yourself back from your baby, perhaps by subscribing to the notion that you must teach her independence now so that your eventual separations will be easier, will hamper the natural process of learning to be her mother. Throw yourself headlong into baby love instead, and you'll soon develop the intuitive knowledge and sensitivity that are essential to a harmonious mother-baby relationship. If I could offer you but one sentence to guide you as you combine motherhood and employment, it would be this: *What matters most is not the number of hours that you and your baby will be together or apart, it is the quality of your attachment with your baby and your confidence in yourself as a mother.*

Breastfeeding in the Early Weeks: The Learning Period

You and your baby will learn to breastfeed over the next six to eight weeks. The ease in which you do so will depend on your baby's temperament and your own understanding of breastfeeding and infant development. Individual babies vary as much as individual adults do; nevertheless, a few milestones are predictable. One is that by eight weeks postpartum breastfeeding will be second nature to both of you.

In the beginning, expect your baby to want to nurse about every two or three hours during the day and a few times during the night.

Generally, new babies nurse 8 to 12 times every 24 hours, without more than four hours passing between feedings. Such frequent feedings are necessary because breast milk is digested rapidly. Nursing as often as your baby wants will keep him content and you comfortable, and will build your milk supply to suit your baby's needs.

You will know your baby is hungry and ready to nurse—*before* he begins wailing—when he roots, turning his head and reaching toward your breast with his chin and mouth and sticking his tongue out or making sucking motions. Offering the breast whenever you see these signs is sometimes called "demand feeding," meaning the baby is fed whenever he wants. A better term would be "request feeding," meaning you don't wait until the desire becomes a demand before satisfying it.

You too can request to nurse if your breasts are feeling especially full. If your baby tends to be very quiet and sleepy during these early weeks, you may need to wake her to nurse more frequently than she would on her own. This can keep you from getting engorged and help maintain your milk supply. Your baby needs these frequent feedings even if she doesn't request them.

As your baby grows she will eventually stretch out the time between nursings and sleep in longer stretches at night. All babies do these things, but on their own individual timetables. If you delay nursings or nurse according to an arbitrary schedule, you may find that your baby is no longer growing as expected, and that he's very unhappy, too.

Milestones during the early weeks include periodic growth spurts. At approximately ten days after birth, at four to six weeks of age, around three months, and again at six months, babies experience sudden and rapid growth. After settling into some semblance of a routine, your baby may one day begin nursing much more frequently. He may seem insatiable. Many a mother has believed (or has been told) that her baby is hungry because she cannot make enough milk for him. But the baby's insatiability will last for just a day or two, until he has stimulated the production of the additional milk he needs to fuel his growth spurt. (Older children do this as well, as parents know who have observed a usually picky eight-year-old suddenly eat everything on his plate and then ask for more.) Your baby manages this simple yet brilliant system with the efficiency of a factory foreman. She sucks in one way to stimulate let-down, in another way to swallow the flood of milk that comes with let-down. She even prepares for her growth spurts by nursing as much as possible to obtain the added energy she will need.

Babies generally experience growth spurts at ten days after birth, at four to six weeks, around three months, and again at six months of age. The sudden change in your baby's appetite at these times may alarm you. Your baby wants to nurse all the time; she acts famished, and fussy, all day long. You may worry that your milk supply has dropped off, and wonder if you should give the baby a bottle of formula. You may fear that this behavior is going to go on forever.

It's not. Your milk supply hasn't fallen off; it's just your baby's needs have suddenly risen. She is nursing more often to build up your milk supply. All you need do is allow your baby and your breasts to readjust to one another by nursing your baby without restriction or supplementation. Of course, you may not get much *else* done for a couple of days as your baby nurses 12 to 18 times in 24 hours, but this is just another part of becoming a mother. (See Chapter 5 for advice on dealing with growth spurts once you are back at work.)

Sometimes a new baby will want to nurse again and again, every 20 to 40 minutes, for two or more hours. Called "cluster feeding," this type of nursing usually occurs at night during the first week or two after birth. After a cluster of feedings, a baby usually falls into a deep sleep. These marathon nursing sessions are nature's way of establishing breastfeeding early on.

The average duration of nursings varies among babies. Babies nurse in different ways, some in one long burst, some intermittently with little rest periods between. Your breasts will adapt to the rhythm of your particular baby, with the milk letting down strongly at first, and then repeatedly or intermittently, according to the baby's sucking patterns. In the early weeks, when your baby is still learning to suck efficiently, he may take quite a long time to withdraw the milk he needs. To avoid sore nipples and engorgement and ensure an ample milk supply, let your baby determine the length of each nursing.

How do you know when your baby is full? He will signal his satiety by relaxing his clenched fists, by giving that sweet little flash of a newborn smile, by releasing the nipple, and often by falling asleep. Or, if your letdown reflex is strong, his tiny tummy may be full (for an hour or so) after nursing on only one breast, and he may refuse the other. If your baby does this, just be sure to offer the full side first at the next feeding.

Even if your baby seems to be asleep, you should offer both breasts at each feeding, starting on the side where the previous feeding ended. Your baby may wake up and nurse again when you switch him to the other side, especially if you burp him in between.

Avoiding Supplements

Supplementary bottles of formula or sugar water can interfere with learning to breastfeed and establishing a milk supply. Healthy breast-fed babies don't need any fluids besides breast milk. They could suppress your baby's appetite, making her less eager for the breast. Also, since artificial nipples require a different way of latching on and sucking, they can confuse the baby who is learning to breastfeed. Fluids flow rapidly through bottle nipples with barely any effort on the part of the baby. If your baby gets accustomed to supplementary bottles in the early days, she may become frustrated and fuss when your milk does not flow the moment she feels your nipple in her mouth. You want your baby to learn to withdraw milk from the breast before she experiences the freer flow of fluid through a bottle nipple. Once breastfeeding is established, you will be able to give your baby a bottle safely (see "Introducing the Bottle," page 112).

How to Tell If Your Baby Is Getting Enough Milk

Mothers' most common concern during these first weeks is whether the baby is getting enough milk. Wouldn't it be nice if our breasts were translucent—if we could see the milk being made, watch as it flows down the ducts to collect in the milk sinuses behind the nipple, and lets down with a gush? Bottle feeding has the psychological advantage that the bottle's contents reassuringly disappear into the baby right before your eyes. Perhaps bottle feeding would never have become so popular if bottles were made of opaque materials. Never mind. You can be sure your baby is getting enough milk if—

- he nurses at least eight times in 24 hours;
- you see and hear him swallowing, after every suck or two;
- after the first week, he has at least eight wet cloth diapers, or three or four very heavy paper ones, in 24 hours (without being given any supplemental water);
- he has clear, pale urine (rather than dark yellow);
- he has one or more bowel movements per day; and
- he gains at least an ounce per day.

Of course, there are always individual variations. After about 6 weeks, a breastfed baby who is getting plenty of milk may not have a bowel movement for a couple of days. Weight gain is also highly individual; some babies may grow in length rather than in weight at first.

Leaking Milk

The first few weeks of breastfeeding can be a rather *wet* time, as your milk leaks and drips and sprays, sometimes when you least expect it. While your baby nurses on one breast, the other breast may leak or even spray milk. This is a wonderful sign—you know then that your let-down reflex is working, even if you don't feel the pins-and-needles sensation that usually occurs when milk lets down (some women never feel this sensation). Your milk may also let down when you are reminded of your baby or of nursing—when someone asks about your baby, when you hear your baby making sounds in her sleep, or even when you just sit down in the chair where you most often nurse your baby. The relaxing warmth of a shower may also stimulate let-down. Over the next few weeks leaking should gradually lessen, though the problem may recur when you go back to work, especially when you are very full or miss a pumping session.

While you're leaking, breast pads of cloth or paper will keep your bra and clothing dry. Reusable, washable cotton pads are the first choice of women who prefer the feel of cloth next to their skin. These pads vary in how much liquid they absorb and how quickly they wick it away from the nipple. Disposable paper pads are also a good choice, although those that are layered with plastic to make them waterproof can keep your nipples moist. (Plastic-lined pads can also slow healing, if your nipples are sore. But if you can't risk leaking while you stand before a jury or wear surgical scrubs, you may definitely prefer plastic-lined pads.) Some disposable pads have an adhesive strip to anchor the pad to the inside of your bra. Others are slit halfway to the center of the pad, so the pad can mold to the shape of your breast. Very thin pads can be layered for extra absorption.

Breast pads are available in drugstores, supermarkets, and baby-supply stores, but to get good cloth ones you may need to order from a baby-care catalog or make your own pads by cutting up diapers.

During this leaky phase you may also need to take a towel into bed with you at night.

Healing Sore Nipples

Nipple soreness, perhaps the most common problem faced by new nursing mothers, ranges from a bit of tenderness to searing pain that can discourage the most committed woman. Usually the cause of the problem is incorrect positioning or sucking. If you are not certain your baby is nursing correctly, call a lactation consultant or a La Leche League leader. She may need to watch you nurse your baby before she can diagnose the problem and help you correct it. Once the problem is identified and corrected, the soreness should disappear within a couple of days.

You can help to prevent or heal sore nipples by keeping them dry and exposed to air as much as possible. If you use breast pads, change them often, and whenever they get wet. A little topless sunbathing, if possible, may help. If you can't go topless even in the house, you can tuck plastic breast shells, plastic domes with holes scattered across the top, in your bra. Available from some La Leche leaders, pharmacies, and baby-supply shops, these devices keep the fabric of your bra or blouse off your nipples and allow air to circulate around them. If milk leaks into the shells, however, your nipples will be bathed in milk, which, kept warm against your body, can breed bacteria. If you wear shells, pour out any milk that accumulates in them, and wash the shells well and frequently.

Although creams and ointments are often recommended to soothe sore nipples, many of these products contain ingredients (including pesticides in some lanolin preparations) that are of questionable safety for your baby if the cream is not completely wiped off before nursing. Many lactation consultants recommend modified (medical grade) lanolin.

The soreness is almost always worst when the baby first latches on, and may lessen as the milk lets down. Always begin nursing on the side that is least sore; nursing on the other side will be less painful after the milk lets down. Nurse frequently, so that your baby does not come to the breast ravenous; a hungry baby can be hard on a sore nipple. Massaging your breasts or using a warm compress as you nurse may help your milk to let down more quickly.

Nursing in a variety of positions can help minimize soreness by distributing the pressure rather than letting it fall on the same part of the nipple at each feeding. In all positions, make sure the baby comes straight onto the breast and that you are holding him close enough and high enough so that he doesn't drag the breast downward or have to tilt or twist his head to nurse.

Your nipples can also be made sore by a thrush infection. Thrush is caused by *Candida albicans,* a fungus that thrives on milk on the nipples, in the milk ducts, and in the baby's mouth. If your nipples suddenly become red and itchy or burning after the first week or more of breastfeeding, you may be dealing with a case of thrush. Other symptoms include cracked nipples and shooting pains in one or both breasts during or after a feeding. If you've got thrush, your baby most likely does, too. She may have white patches on the inside of her cheeks or lips or on the tongue, or a diaper rash. She may nurse reluctantly or with an altered suck because her mouth is sore.

If you suspect you have a thrush infection, see you doctor. She may prescribe liquid nystatin for your baby's mouth and nystatin cream for your nipples and areola. Continue treatment for two weeks, even though the symptoms will be gone in as little as a day or, at the most, five days. Change and wash your breast pads after every feeding in hot, soapy water, and boil them every day for a few minutes. Rinse your nipples after nursing, and wash your hands frequently to avoid reinfection. You should of course keep nursing throughout the infection and its treatment; if nursing is too painful, pump the affected breast with a fully automatic breast pump.

Preventing and Treating Plugged Ducts and Breast Infections

If you notice a tender place in your breast, one that is especially sore when you press on it, it is very probably a plugged duct. Plugged ducts are less common than sore nipples, but can be even more discouraging. They are caused when a milk duct does not drain completely and the milk backs up and forms a plug. The plug puts pressure on the tissue around it, which becomes inflamed and sore. If the plug is not loosened, it may become infected. Often a plugged duct seem to be nature's way of saying, "You're doing too much. You need to rest *now*."

Plugged ducts are truly tiresome. The best remedy however, is not weaning but frequent nursing—at least every 2 hours for 24 hours or as long as the breast is tender. If you can, go straight to bed—*with* your baby. Start every feeding on the affected side, and vary the positions in which you nurse. Lactation consultants advise nursing the baby in a position that points his chin at the sore spot ("even if you have to stand on your head to do it," says one lactation consultant); that spot will receive the most suction. Just pulling your baby's knees tight against your tummy will help, by evening the pressure against your breast. Put warm compresses or a heating pad on the sore place, and massage the area gently while it is warm, pressing the lump toward your nipple. You are trying to knead the duct open so that the backed-up milk can flow freely again. Sometimes a plug is in a nipple pore; you may see dried secretions come out as a spaghetti-like strand or as dry, sandy bits. Either breastfeed your baby or pump your milk on the affected side immediately after massaging to further clear the plug. Taking the day off to rest, nurse frequently, and treat your breast with heat and gentle massage may well prevent a bout of mastitis.

The Instaheat Pad is a nifty remedy for plugged ducts and mastitis. Made by Medela, the sealed plastic bag is filled with sodium acetate and water and contoured to fit into a bra over a sore spot. Bend the bag to set off a chemical reaction that causes the fluid inside to become hot. The Instaheat Pad is available for about twenty dollars at maternity shops.

If you have a very painful spot in your breast (one that is red, warm, and hard), if you have a fever, and if you feel as though you are getting the flu, you can be almost certain that you have developed a breast infection, or mastitis. If the fever is high or has lasted for more than 24 hours, you may need antibiotics. Call your doctor. Be cautious, however, if the doctor advises you to stop nursing until the infection is gone or until you have finished the course of antibiotics (do take the entire course). Continuing to nurse during mastitis will not harm your baby: The antibodies in your milk protect your baby from any bacteria. Frequent nursing, especially on the affected side, is essential to clear the duct. Mastitis tends to cause a mother's milk supply to drop, making her baby want to nurse almost constantly, which is the best treatment of all. The mastitis would certainly be aggravated if your breast became engorged, as it surely would if you abruptly weaned your baby. (Mastitis gone one step further is a breast abscess, or a localized collection of pus, that must be surgically drained.) The antibiotic your doctor prescribes should be safe for your baby; ask your doctor to verify that it is. As with plugged ducts, going to bed immediately with your baby to rest and nurse as much as possible will help you to overcome mastitis and prevent it from returning.

Occasionally a baby is reluctant to nurse on an infected breast. If this is the case with your baby, offer the affected breast first when he is very hungry, asleep, or very sleepy. Try different nursing positions, or nurse him while walking or swaying. Mastitis can also make the areola hard, and difficult for the baby to grasp. To soften the areola, express a little milk before you nurse. You may need to pump the affected breast while continuing to nurse the baby from it as much as possible (a baby can withdraw milk more effectively than a pump can).

To prevent plugged ducts and mastitis, you must understand how and why plugged ducts develop in the first place. They tend to occur when a feeding is missed, nursing is irregular, or the breasts are incompletely drained. Sometimes a woman takes great care to rest a lot and nurse often during the first two weeks at home, but then, when she feels ready to get out of the house and do more things, she does them with a vengeance, spending all day out and about. Not only does she nurse a little less than the day before, but she may tire herself out as well. And the next morning she wakes up with a sore breast and, perhaps, a fever.

Ease back into your slate of activities gradually, keeping track of how often you're putting the baby to the breast. Anything that causes you to nurse less frequently can leave you dealing with a plugged duct. This can include your baby's sleeping for a longer stretch at night, introducing supplementary bottles, using a pacifier, or the hullabaloo surrounding holidays and house guests.

Incorrect positioning and poor latch-on and sucking, which so often cause sore nipples, can also lead to plugged ducts, by preventing your milk from flowing freely. If you suspect any one of these could be the cause of your plugged ducts or mastitis, call a lactation consultant or a La Leche League leader for one-on-one assistance. You want to be sure that your baby is draining at least one breast completely at each feeding.

Plugs can also be caused by anything that restricts the flow of milk in your breasts, including wearing an ill-fitting bra, carrying a heavy purse or diaper bag on your shoulder, or carrying the baby in a front pack or in any manner that puts pressure on your breasts. Avoid wearing underwire bras, and go braless as much as possible, or at least switch to a bra a size larger than you normally wear. Sleeping on your abdomen may also cause a plug.

Stress and fatigue can lead to plugged ducts, too. And since your resistance to infection is lower when you are under stress, any plugged duct you get while you are feeling stressed or exhausted is more likely to lead to an infection. Traditions in other cultures that enable new mothers to rest and be taken care of for a month or more usually prevent plugged ducts and mastitis.

For mothers who do not plan to return to work, plugged ducts and mastitis are generally a thing of the past by the third month. Working mothers, however, may find themselves dealing with them all over again, or for the very first time, during their first weeks back at work. The causes are the same: an abrupt decrease in nursing frequency, incomplete emptying of the breasts, restrictive clothing, stress and fatigue. Again, being aware of the causes will enable you to rid yourself of plugged ducts and mastitis in short order.

Mastitis will recur if it hasn't fully cleared up the first time around, and it sometimes becomes a chronic problem. If you take antibiotics, be sure to finish the prescription, and to get extra rest for a good two weeks afterward.

If you have one bout of plugged ducts or mastitis after another, consider these questions:

- Are you getting enough fluids? Whether you are plagued by plugs or not, as a nursing mother you should be drinking a lot of fluids. Some women keep a liter water bottle with them at all times.
- Is your diet high in saturated fat? Some mothers say that limiting fat intake—even just switching from whole to skim milk—has dramatically helped them with recurrent plugged ducts.
- Are you using too much or too little salt? Excessive salt intake and chronic salt deficiency can both contribute to recurring mastitis.

Once identified, all potential causes of mastitis can be eliminated.

Carrying Your Baby

Answering newborn's needs all day long can be inconvenient if not exhausting. What do you do if your baby cries every time you put him down? How do you brush your teeth? How do you get anything done at all? In societies where women's domestic activities are essential to the survival of their families and, indeed, their communities, work does not cease when a baby is born. These mothers wear their babies in slings or wrapped on their hips or their backs. Their hands are free to do the things that need to be done, while their babies are usually peaceful, contented companions.

In one study, babies who were carried most of the day cried 43

All over the world, women know that their babies are happier and that it is easier to do their work when they carry their babies.

percent less than others. Why is a baby who is carried so much more content than one who is not? Babies born today are just the same as babies born thousands of years ago, long before carriages, cribs, and bouncy seats. They represent our three-million-year-old mammalian heritage unaltered. Humans are not birds or reptiles who leave their babies in nests while they forage for food. Nor are we like hunting mammals, who leave their young in hidden lairs and return to nurse at widely spaced intervals. We are a "carrying" species, like apes and certain other mammals who keep our young with us while we work, eat, and sleep. We need to keep our babies close so we can nurse them often because our milk is low in fat compared to the milk of many other mammals. This is why a baby is born with a well-developed grasping reflex; it is intended to help him to hold on to his mother's body or hair. Like the sucking reflex, the grasping reflex is fully operational at birth because it was essential for our ancestors' survival.

The baby who is carried simply feels *right*. Infants crave motion. Ethologist Irenäus Eibl-Eibesfeldt observes that "mothers fondle their children in all cultures, lift them up or rock them in slumber. The rocking, jostling, and lifting of infants, which mothers enjoy doing so much, accommodates the infantile need for vestibular stimulation. An excited infant can be calmed by rocking it. Vestibular stimuli communicate to the infant that he is not alone."

> "As a fetus grows in the womb, surrounded by amniotic fluid, it feels liquid warmth, the heartbeat, the inner surf of the mother, and floats in a wonderful hammock that rocks gently as she walks. Birth must be a rude shock after such serenity, and a mother recreates the comfort of the womb in various ways (swaddling, cradling, pressing the baby against the left side of her body where her heart is)."
>
> —DIANE ACKERMAN

The baby who is carried spends his days much as he did in the womb. The familiar roll of his mother's stride, her soothing voice, and her heartbeat are all still constant. Carrying your baby allows him to spend these early months in a sort of fourth trimester, a comfortable transition to all that is to come.

Being carried prepares your baby for his future as well as reminding him of his recent past. He can make eye contact with everyone around. Although he can sleep or nurse whenever he needs to, when he is alert he is a part of his mother's world, watching everything and joining in as soon as he is able. Said one mother, after carrying her four-month-old in a sling for the first time while cooking dinner, "The fun thing was how interested he was in everything I was doing. When I turned on the kitchen faucet he would reach for the water. When I opened the refrigerator, he peered inside. He watched fascinated as I cut veggies."

Carrying your baby won't make him clingy and unable to separate from you as he grows. Babies who are allowed to grow toward independence at their own pace are likely to achieve it earlier and more solidly than if they are hurried toward it. Among the Yequana Indians of South America, who carried their babies until they climbed down and crawled away, Jean Leidloff found the children precociously and astonishingly self-reliant. But exactly when your baby is ready to spend more time out of your arms will depend on his temperament. A baby born with a high need for tactile stimulation may prefer to be in a sling or pack until he starts to crawl, or even longer. A different baby may feel quite ready at three months to lie on a blanket watching a shaft of sunlight while you make breakfast.

When you are out and about, slings, frontpacks, and backpacks give you far more mobility than a stroller, which turns every door, stair, and narrow space into an obstacle to negotiate or avoid. They also keep your hands free to cook, write, sow seeds, pick up the phone, open the mail, walk in the woods, or hold the hand of another child. By carrying your baby as mothers always have, you can meet your baby's needs and continue with all the activities of daily life at the same time.

Most importantly, carrying your baby vastly increases the amount of daily contact between you. When you do return to work, the extended contact provided by carrying your baby during the hours you are at home will offset the effects of your daily separations. Indeed, frequent physical contact and interaction with your baby boosts your body's production of prolactin, which has been called the mothering hormone.

Fathers report that they, too, enjoy carrying their babies in slings and baby packs. The close physical contact a sling or baby pack enables a father to have with his baby gives them both a deep familiarity with the sound and scent and motions of the other. They will *know* each other far more than the father and baby who spend half an hour visiting a couple of times a day.

You can make or buy a sling or baby pack in any of numerous styles. Frontpacks are useful with small babies. Some models allow the baby to face forward so she can look out at the world. Most backpacks are best suited for older babies. Dads, especially, love backpacks for long strolls. They tend to put less strain on the shoulders and neck than frontpacks do, and they are safer to use while cooking in the kitchen.

A sling that drapes across your shoulder and around the opposite hip snuggles your baby—head, arms, legs, and all—in much the same comforting way the womb or a well-wrapped blanket does. A sling is also a cinch to take on and off; you don't need someone else's help to buckle it or to put the baby in. A sling also allows you to nurse discreetly in public; who can tell if the baby is sleeping or nursing when all one can see is the sling? Best of all, say mothers, is that if your baby falls asleep in the sling you can lay her down without waking her up simply by leaning over and sliding backwards out of the sling. She'll stay just as blissfully snuggled as she was when she first fell asleep. A sling can be used from birth to about three years (35 to 40 pounds)— much longer than a frontpack. Not only is a sling more comfortable

Babies can lie down or sit up, and face forward or backward, while in a sling.

and versatile for a growing baby than a frontpack, but it will be far more comfortable for you as time goes by, because it places the weight of your baby on your hips rather than on your shoulders.

A sling can feel awkward at first, but in time it will be easier to use than a frontpack or backpack. You may want to practice with a stuffed animal or doll before putting your baby in the sling. But do get your baby accustomed to the sling as early as possible.

Most commercially available slings have a padded square to rest on your shoulder and a ring and pull-tab for adjusting the length of the sling. You can make your own sling out of sturdy fabric 1½ yards long; tie a strong knot at your shoulder. To carry your baby in a sling—

- Lift it over your head, and place the padded square (or knot) on the edge of your shoulder. The ring and pull-tab on a commercially made sling should be in front of your shoulder. The sling should now hang across your body.
- Fluff out the fabric.
- Balance your baby on your right shoulder (the one without the strap), and guide his feet into the sling. If your baby is a newborn, he should be fully swaddled in the fabric.
- If your baby is very small, you might fold a thin baby blanket or cloth diaper into a square, and tuck it under his head and shoulders for a little additional support.
- To cinch up a commercially made sling, lift the baby's weight with one hand, and pull on the tab with the other hand.
- Walk with a little jiggle and pat the baby's bottom a bit to settle him in the sling.

Your baby will probably be happiest if you lay him in the sling with his head to your left. Eighty percent of all mothers tend to carry their children on the left side (the side on which the sling is on your shoulder). Look at paintings and sculptures created through the centuries, and you will see that this has always been true the world over. This phenomenon has been thought to be due to the prevalence of right-handedness, since carrying the baby on the left frees the mother's right hand. But left-handed mothers also tend to carry their babies on the left side.

Researchers have observed that newborns, when gently held facing forward, display clear preferences for turning their heads to one side or the other. About two-thirds of babies turn their heads to the right. (When they are held on the mother's left side, then, they turn to

Slings are easy to put on and take off.

A sling enables you to nurse your baby wherever you are and whatever you may be doing.

face her breast to hear the beat of her heart). The other third, however, tend to turn to the left—and, researchers have found, their mothers tend to carry them on the *right*. You may already be carrying your baby on the side that reflects her innate preference. If your baby turns her head to the left and you tend to carry her on the right, put the sling's strap on your right shoulder.

When they are three or four months old, many babies like to sit up and look out at the world. This is when you might let your baby's legs dangle out at the front of the sling. Make sure the batting on the lower edge of a commercially made sling fully supports her knees and bottom. Or you can turn the baby around to sit cross-legged, so she faces the oncoming world. This position, as one mother says, is "very exciting for babies and little old ladies in the supermarket." As your baby gains control of her head, she will want to sit up in the sling more and more, straddling your hips with her legs, her bottom supported by the sling. With practice you will find that you can carry your baby on your back in the sling, which is especially useful when chopping vegetables in the kitchen or working at the computer.

Don't give up on the sling if your baby fusses at first; keep using it for a few days to let both of you grow accustomed to it. As with nursing, once you get the hang of a sling you will be able to use it anywhere, anytime.

Older babies enjoy facing forward and looking out at the world when being carried.

*By carrying your baby, you can carry on with all your daily activities
while meeting your baby's need for contact with you.*

If you aren't enjoying using a sling or baby pack, or your baby isn't, remember that carrying your baby, like breastfeeding, is just one of the tools of attachment in our human heritage. You don't need to carry your baby every second of every day to ensure that you and he develop a strong and harmonious bond. But if you find yourself hesitating to pick up your baby when he cries, or if someone tells you that "you're spoiling that baby by carrying him so much," remember that babies have always been picked up when they fuss and carried about by their mothers. Babies are still as they have always been; it is only adults who have changed.

Where Will Your Baby Sleep?

Sleepless nights are a hallmark of the newborn period. Your baby's admirers quickly follow "How old is she?" and "How much does she weigh?" with "Is she sleeping through the night yet?" Getting your baby to sleep through the night (whatever that means) is requisite to being a "good mother" (whatever *that* means). Mothers who are planning their return to work may feel desperate to ensure full nights of sleep as soon as possible.

There are as many schools of thought on how to get babies to sleep all night as there are on the proper feeding of babies. One especially popular technique of late is to let the baby cry in her crib for increasingly long periods of time each night. The program does seem to work. In fairly short order, the babies trained in this way don't cry at night anymore. They have learned that no matter how much they cry, their wails won't be answered. They have reached a state behavioral researchers term "learned hopelessness." No long-term studies have been done on these babies, but one cannot help but wonder if they will form a lifelong pessimistic outlook, for these early lessons are not easily unlearned.

Many parents reject these baby-care fads. They have looked at the ways in which babies are cared for in most of the world, and have decided that the Western taboo against letting babies sleep in their parents' beds doesn't make any sense. These parents have discovered that, when they bring their babies into their own beds to sleep, everyone sleeps better. A new father admits with some amazement, "We didn't start out with a family bed. In fact, we were rather adamant that our son sleep in his own crib. But after weeks of getting up for feedings or getting up to check on the baby or getting up because the monitor was crackling, we decided to try having him sleep with us full time. It worked great! We got *more* sleep and our son seemed to sleep better, and to be more secure, too."

The practice of sending newborns from the womb to the solitude of a crib in a separate room is unique to modern Western culture. There is a story that Margaret Mead, the anthropologist, was asked by Samoan mothers if it was true that "American mothers make their babies sleep in cages at night." Imagine the experience from the newborn's point of view, and you can see why these mothers were so bewildered by our use of cribs. Unaware even that he is a separate person from his mother, the baby finds himself without her in the vast, still openness of a crib. His instincts tell him it is dangerous to be alone in the dark, away from people and where wolves might find him. Utterly helpless, he panics. No wonder babies cry at night.

> *"One vital quality of privacy is that we take it when we choose, otherwise it's called loneliness."*
>
> —DEBORAH JACKSON

Nature intends for your baby to nurse at night. Because breast milk is quickly digested, newborns are normally hungry every two or three hours around the clock. Your prolactin levels are highest between 1:00 A.M. and 5:00 A.M., and your milk has a higher fat content at night. If you don't nurse enough at night, your breasts will be too full every morning, which will lower your total milk production.

If your baby spends the night alone, he must wake fully when he is hungry, and cry long and loud enough for you to hear him in your sleep. You too must wake fully, leave your bed and go to his room, pick him up, settle in a chair to nurse, then nurse him, rock him back to sleep, and ever so carefully place him back in his crib without waking him up. Only then can you return to your bed and get yourself back to sleep. You must repeat this every two or three hours all night long. (Imagine adding a trip to the kitchen to prepare a bottle of formula to all that nocturnal activity!)

Consider the difference if your baby sleeps alongside you in your bed. He begins to snuffle and make sucking motions in his sleep. You wake just enough to draw him close to your breast without sitting up. He latches on and nurses without ever crying or waking completely. As he nurses, you fall back into a light sleep. When he is satiated, he falls back into a deep sleep. Neither of you has woken fully, and you both feel comforted because the other is near. Your mate sleeps soundly on the other side of the bed, usually unaware of your ministrations. (What about changing your baby's diaper? Unless he is really soaked and leaking, don't bother until morning.)

Sleeping with your baby, like picking your baby up when he cries, teaches him trust. He learns in the most fundamental way that he is safe and well loved. He knows that you are always there for him, that you will be there for him when he stumbles, and this knowledge frees him to grow toward independence. He forms a sense of what child psychologist Erik Erikson called "basic trust"; he can safely risk growing up.

Most important for you as a working mother, sharing your bed with your baby gives you an additional eight to nine hours a day in which you and he are in close contact. The two of you interact a great deal in the night, even though most of the time you're not fully conscious.

Sharing your bed with your baby also prepares you for the possibility of reverse-cycle feeding. Some babies whose mothers are away five or more hours a day tend to sleep more during the day than other babies and to stay awake, socialize, and nurse more in the evenings and at night. When Mom is not around, the baby saves his energy. But when reunited with Mom, the baby more than makes up for the hours apart. This is a lovely and touching adjustment, a tribute a baby pays to his beloved mother. Sharing your bed with your baby makes it possible for you to accept this natural adjustment and still get the rest you need.

Allowing your baby to nurse at night will also maintain your milk supply while you are working. A baby who reverses his cycle of rest and activity may not drink all of the pumped breast milk Mom has left at the sitter's; he is getting most of the nourishment he needs during the time he is with his mother, and would rather wait for her to provide his meals, thank you very much. If you're nursing a lot at night, you may be able to give up pumping your milk sooner than otherwise. See Chapter 6 for tips on encouraging your baby to adopt reverse-cycle feeding, if he doesn't do so on his own.

Many parents would be happy to bring their babies into bed with them if they weren't concerned about rolling over on the baby while sleeping. Don't worry; you won't. Remember that parents the world over sleep safely with their babies. In fact, the tragedy of Sudden Infant

Death Syndrome (SIDS) rarely occurs in societies where all babies sleep with their mothers. Perhaps, as some researchers theorize, mothers and babies who sleep together unconsciously synchronize their breathing. A baby with an immature nervous system may be kept breathing in a regular pattern by the steady, close, strong breathing of his mother.

Other parents worry about the baby falling off the bed or smothering in the bedding. Your baby will be safe between you and your mate so long as the baby's head and face are clear of your pillows. (Waterbeds, however, are not safe for babies.) If you want to be free to snuggle with your mate, you can put the baby between you and the edge of the bed; just push the bed tightly against a wall or use a portable bed rail (available at any store that sells children's furniture). If you would rather not have your baby right in your bed, you can push a crib against your bed with one side removed, in a sort of sidecar arrangement. A bassinet or cradle by the side of your bed is another alternative to a crib in a separate room.

Once you let your baby into your bed, you may wonder, will he ever leave? Babies eventually wean themselves of their parents' bed just as they do of their mothers' milk, although you can hurry along the process if you like. Some couples love waking up with a cuddly two-year-old; others move the baby into a bed of his own at six months. Either way, when the transition is made gradually and with love, your baby will eventually learn to sleep securely in his own bed. (Snazzy new sheets printed with favorite cartoon characters or fire trucks have been known to work wonders with toddlers.) You may find that, long after your child has begun sleeping in his own bed, he still makes his way to yours when he needs you—when he has had a bad dream, when he is sick, or when he is feeling stressed by some events in his life. Again, seeking you out in the night is not a discipline problem; it is a measure of the depth of your attachment.

What about your privacy? Frankly, most of it was lost the moment your baby was born—and you are unlikely to get it back until your youngest child leaves home. But what little privacy you have can be found in places other than your bed. Many parents keep part of the night to themselves by rocking and nursing the baby to sleep at bedtime, putting him in the crib until he wakes, then bringing him into their bed when he wakes a few hours later.

Caring for Yourself

No matter how you choose to nurture your baby, you will find it hard going unless you nurture yourself as well. In the first eight weeks following your baby's birth, take extra care to be sure that you are resting enough and eating well. Not only are you making tremendous emotional adjustments, but your body is nourishing another human being, besides recovering from the stress of giving birth and reverting to its prepregnant state. Getting too little rest at this time can lead to problems that can quickly snowball into a miserable situation that may include mastitis, breastfeeding failure, or depression. Obey the cardinal rule of the postpartum period: Sleep when the baby sleeps. If your baby falls asleep while nursing, stretch out where you are, if possible, and, with your baby still in your arms or lying on your chest, take a nap. Even a twenty-minute catnap can do wonders for your well-being.

> *If you are standing, sit. If you are sitting, lie down. If you are lying down, sleep. These guidelines become imperatives if you have given birth by cesarean section.*

Pay close attention to your nutritional needs during these postpartum weeks. Nursing mothers are usually thirsty and eager to drink copious amounts of fluids. Let your mate know that one of the most helpful things he can do for you while he is home is to be sure that you always have a large glass of water or juice next to you when you sit down to nurse. You may feel intensely thirsty the moment your milk lets down; in this way nature reminds you that you need fluids. (You needn't drown yourself in fluids, though. Just drink when you're thirsty.) If you don't drink a lot of milk normally, however, don't feel as though you must drink it now. You don't need to drink cow's milk to make human milk. Cow's milk is a convenient source of necessary protein and calcium, but both nutrients can be found in a lot of other foods. Indeed, too much cow's milk in your diet may make your baby uncomfortable. A very occasional glass of wine or beer is probably not harmful and may even encourage your let-down by helping you to relax (midwives traditionally recommended ale for nursing mothers). Alcohol does pass through breast milk to the baby, however, so moderation is essential.

This is not the time to go on a weight-loss diet. Breastfeeding women generally lose the extra weight they put on in pregnancy without any special effort. In fact, many mothers say that as long as they are nursing they can dig into their meals with gusto, taking second helpings and adding dollops of cream, without gaining a pound. It has long been believed that a nursing mother needs about 500 calories more each day than she did before pregnancy to cover the energy requirements of lactation, but a recent study disputes this. The sensible advice is to eat when you are hungry and not beyond satiation.

The quality of your breast milk does not depend on the quality of the food you eat; your milk-producing glands will raid your body for any vitamins, minerals, or protein missing from your diet but needed for milk production. So although you can now eat more than you used to, this does not mean that you should fill up on "cheat foods" such as cake and sweet rolls. If you do, you won't lose weight, and you'll tend to feel tired and "used up." While you are breastfeeding, especially during the first weeks postpartum, you need extra protein and extra calcium. Tuck into well-balanced meals of beans, meat, chicken, cheese, eggs, or fish; fresh fruits and green or orange vegetables; and brown rice, whole-grain breads, or cereals. Stock the refrigerator and cupboards with nourishing foods you can prepare quickly, especially ones high in protein. You're less likely to skimp, or to fill up on doughnuts, if something better is within easy reach. Quick-cooking oatmeal, hard-boiled eggs, nuts, canned tuna, baked or refried beans, and tofu all make nearly instant, nutritious snacks or meals. Your baby will be fine whatever you eat, but you will feel better if you eat good food, and plenty of it, during the first few weeks.

If your physician prescribed a multivitamin and iron supplement while you were pregnant, continue taking it as long as you are nursing. If you are not taking a multivitamin, you may want to take a daily B-complex supplement since a lack of B vitamins can cause depression and anxiousness. Brewer's yeast, a natural source of B vitamins, iron, and protein, is very good for nursing mothers—another reason midwifes recommended dark ale.

Although breastfeeding generally doesn't limit a mother's diet in any way, sometimes a young baby will fuss for a day or so after his mother has eaten a specific food. Common culprits are caffeine, cow's milk and dairy products, chocolate, onions, cabbage, broccoli, brussels sprouts, cauliflower, beans, garlic, cinnamon, tomatoes, and citrus fruits. Most babies wouldn't mind a bit if their mothers made an entire meal of these foods. But if your baby is very fussy one day, suddenly refuses to nurse, has gas or diarrhea, or has a rash or redness around the anus, review your diet over the past 24 hours. You will want to rule out other possible causes, of course, but if you think something you ate is at fault, eliminate from your diet for two to three days any food you suspect, perhaps because you or someone else in your family is sensitive to it. If your baby's troubles are caused by something in your diet, he is likely to fuss two to eight hours after you have ingested it. Most food sensitivities vanish when a baby is about three months old.

Simplification

You can create a more restful atmosphere in your home by simplifying your life wherever and whenever possible. The cliché that something worth doing is worth doing well just isn't true, at least not at this stage in your life. Right now, if something is barely worth doing, then barely do it. Review your housekeeping standards and decide how you can reduce your chores in ways that won't make a discernible difference (or *can* be discerned, but who cares?). For example—

- Arrange for someone else to clean your home, or be satisfied with shortcut cleaning.
- Leave the breakfast dishes (all right, and the lunch and dinner dishes, too) soaking in the sink until you are good and ready to do them. Better yet, use paper plates.
- Make simple meals, and indulge in nutritious take-out food.
- Ask a friend who cooks well for a week's worth of meals that can be frozen, in place of a present for the baby.
- Use disposable diapers, or sign up with a diaper service.
- Vacuum the middle of the room, but skip going under the sofa. (Or don't vacuum at all. Imagine that!)
- Leave socks in a basket to be retrieved as needed rather than sorting and putting them away.
- Unclutter your house so that you have less to clean; box up all those knickknacks for the next five years.
- Use a telephone-answering machine to screen calls.
- Say no as much as possible to requests and intrusions.
- Use a portable phone so you can answer the phone without getting up.

You'll want to extend these simplification measures through the first year or more after you return to work. They are as helpful to working mothers as they are to mothers of newborns.

Enlisting Help from Your Mate

Somehow, when a woman becomes responsible for every need of her baby, she also becomes responsible for every need of her family. Perhaps your division of duties before the baby was born was completely egalitarian. Your mate cooked dinner; you mowed the lawn. You washed and dried the laundry; he folded it and put it away. But even the most modern and fair arrangements tend to become more traditional when a baby enters the equation.

To prevent being saddled with all the cooking, cleaning, and other jobs that your home life requires (or to unsaddle yourself), enlist your mate's help, and applaud his efforts. You are far more likely to get him to do what you need with praise than with criticism. And once he is doing the minimum you need (coming home at a reasonable hour, doing a few loads of laundry), he is more likely to take on additional responsibilities if he knows that you are pleased with his efforts so far.

Keep in mind that your mate's idea of an adequate meal or a clean room may differ from yours. The continual inadequacy of men's housework can be infuriating to women; as a result, many men feel that there is no point in offering to do things, since their wives always get mad and tell them they've done it wrong. If you praise your mate's efforts, they are more likely to improve and become proud and established skills. Help from your mate with the household now will enable you to focus on learning to breastfeed and getting to know your baby. His help when you return to work may make the difference between successfully blending work and home or becoming utterly exhausted by your dual roles.

Feeling Blue and Finding Support

New motherhood can jostle your emotional life whether you plan to return to work or not. Mood swings, sudden inexplicable tears, and feeling vulnerable and overwhelmed are common during the first six weeks. They're known as the baby blues, and a mother's susceptibility to them generally peaks at the third day after birth (about when the milk comes in) and subsides about two to three weeks after birth. Maybe we tend to feel rocky during these early weeks because we so often give birth and care for our newborns in biologically bizarre circumstances—alone or among strangers, and without experienced mothers to guide us. Shifting hormone levels also play a role, but if you're lacking emotional support you should seek some out. Attend a La Leche League meeting or a reunion of your childbirth class. Sign up for a mother-baby exercise class to meet other new mothers. Check the bulletin boards at your public library and local churches for notices of new mothers' groups forming, or form one yourself. Seek out especially other nursing mothers who plan to return to work, and talk with mothers at your workplace who were supportive during your pregnancy. Sharing your concerns with other parents is more than practical; it is sustenance for your soul. As someone who has devoted much of her time and energy to work, you may now need to build a network of home- and child-focused friends. Doing so does not mean you are losing your old life and friends; you are only expanding your circle to include people who can share this new stage in your life. The friends you make through your children will be the ones who are there for you when you desperately need a babysitter or a ride to the emergency room. They will be your source of recommendations for a doctor, dentist, school, or place to find used ice skates.

If you have a computer and a modem, seek out other parents in cyberspace. You can find computer forums, or conversations by modem, on every conceivable subject related to parenting: newborns, breastfeeding, working mothers, attachment parenting, single mothers, egalitarian parenting, executive mothers, and more. The messages shared in these forums make fascinating reading. Every problem you are facing or might face in the future is likely to be discussed by forum participants. Ask for advice on sore nipples, sleepless nights, finding day care, or choosing a breast pump, and you are likely to receive a dozen helpful and empathetic responses from parents who have been in your precise situation. One mother echoed many when she wrote, "Thank goodness for this board and for all of you. I don't know how I would have gotten through the last few weeks without it." You may find Internet sites helpful, too; popular sites for parents and working women are listed in "Resources."

Simple activities can dramatically lift your mood as well. For example—

- Take a daily walk in the afternoon sun with the baby tucked in a sling or frontpack. The fresh air and exercise will do you both good.

- Walk to a nearby playground; you'll probably find other parents to commiserate and rejoice with.
- Go to a mall just to window-shop and people-watch.
- If you feel like crying, let your tears flow. The shower is a great place to sob unselfconsciously. Cry out loud right along with your baby; you're certain to feel better when you are done.
- Buy a new outfit that is comfortable, easy to nurse in, and pretty, too.
- Take a long bath while your mate holds the baby, or take a bath *with* your baby.
- Rent a funny movie to watch while you are nursing.
- Call someone who makes you laugh.
- While you nurse, read *Operating Instructions,* Anne Lamott's hilarious and insightful memoir of her son's first year. If you can't manage a full-length book right now, try *A Teeny Tiny Baby,* Amy Schwartz's brilliant, tender, and very funny picture book for children.

Practice nursing in new places around your home and while doing something else simultaneously: reading, writing letters, or talking on the phone.

If your baby blues seem more than mild—if you feel so sad that you are nearly immobilized—you may be experiencing postpartum depression. True postpartum depression usually begins three weeks to five months after birth. Professional help is essential; see "Resources."

When you feel overwhelmed and anxious, remember that your feelings are normal. They do not mean that you are better suited to your life at work than to life as a mother. If you have always placed a priority on feeling in charge, try to put aside that need during these weeks as you open yourself up to motherhood. You may be considering cutting short your maternity leave or hiring a baby nurse in an attempt to regain control and return your life to normality, but doing so would only slow your adjustment to motherhood and put a distance between you and your baby. The first few weeks on any new job feel chaotic and overwhelming; motherhood is no different.

Although right now this lifetime commitment you've made fills every minute of every day, it won't always be so. Your baby will not always want to nurse every two hours, and you will not always be bleary-eyed and in your pajamas. You *will* figure out not only how to accomplish a shower and lunch in the same day, but how to get your baby and yourself dressed and out the door by 8:00 A.M. In fact, with time, the organizational and coping skills you gain as a mother will reach astonishing heights—skills that you are likely to find yourself applying to your professional work as well. Meanwhile, nursing will become your source of peace and release, providing tranquil departures from the clamoring demands of the world. And your baby, your partner in a mutually rewarding relationship, will serve as your ally in blending your many roles into one harmonious whole.

CHAPTER 5

PREPARING TO GO BACK TO WORK

"I can't imagine leaving my baby now."

WHETHER YOUR EARLIEST WEEKS as a mother are smooth or rough going, a day will certainly come when everything suddenly seems a little easier. You've learned a lot about your baby by the end of the first four to six weeks. You know when he is hungry, you can tell when he needs to sleep, you have a repertoire of ways to comfort him. If you go to the supermarket without him, you miss him within twenty minutes and hurry to get home again. You have left the initial learning period behind and have entered the reward period, when breastfeeding and caring for your baby are much less perplexing and even a lot of fun.

Whereas mothers who plan to stay home indefinitely can relax at this point and thoroughly enjoy their babies, your mind may be on the rapidly approaching day when you will return to work. You've entered a stage that is unique to working mothers. In some ways this period feels like those last weeks of pregnancy; it is marked by anticipation, anxiety, and the sense that you don't really know what's waiting for you just around the corner.

Working mothers experience a wide range of emotions at this

time. Much depends on how you feel about your work. Do you love it? If so, you may be eager to be back at it, or you may feel a bittersweet tug in two directions. Do you work just for the money and benefits, and would you quit if you could? If so, you may be feeling especially stressed at this time. Whether you are grief-stricken or raring to go, the intensity of your feelings in this period is entirely normal. You've hit the rapids, the whitecaps and whirlpools where two rivers converge, in the lives of women at the verge of the twenty-first century. There are no time-honored traditions to guide us here; each of us finds her own way through these waters.

Maybe you feel comfortable with your decision to work but worry about the logistics. You may still find it a challenge to get yourself and your baby out of the house and to the supermarket by noon. How will you get the baby to day care and yourself to work by nine o'clock every morning? How will you attend that out-of-town sales conference two months from now without weaning your baby? The questions hover like biting flies.

Take this first year of motherhood one day at a time. Know that your abilities will expand with the demands you put upon them—not infinitely, but farther than you might ever have thought possible. Try to brush away worrying questions for now. One of the lessons of motherhood is that you needn't plan everything in fixed detail, because your plans are likely to be disrupted anyway. Trust that you will figure out the right thing to do when you need to do it. Know that solutions will evolve, that you will find answers when you need them. Mothering can teach you to ride life instead of directing it, to be open to unexpected opportunities and ready for sudden turns in the road. You will learn to respond to the rest of your life as spontaneously and intuitively as you do to your baby's cues and needs.

Whether you are looking forward to going back to your job or dreading it, know that you have already put into place the element most important to your success in blending your working life and your home life: your attachment to your baby. A strong attachment will prevent the hours you spend apart from disturbing the harmony of your relationship and interfering with the development of your nurturing skills. Continue to care for your baby as you began, using the tools in your parenting toolbox: breastfeeding the baby and responding quickly to her cues, and carrying her about and sleeping with her if these work for you. These ancient ways of mothering can help you ensure that you and your baby will stay in harmony despite your daily separations and the distractions of work. Breastfeeding in particular will not only keep you and your baby close, but it will supply you with constant, reassuring evidence of your unique place at the center of your baby's world.

Reconnecting with the Outside World

Since you gave birth, you may have put aside all thought of the world beyond the baby in your arms. Once you may not have believed that your world could become so contracted; now it may be hard to imagine leaving the cozy cocoon of your home. If so, your first task may be to restretch your boundaries so that you feel comfortable and confident in the outside world. You can begin simply by nursing in new places around your home or while you are doing something else—

Learn to nurse your baby while working, if possible.

working at the computer or talking on the phone. Try nursing at a friend's house. Move on to nursing in a restaurant or in a changing room at a clothing shop. When you're really comfortable, try a park bench.

Nursing in public may be a hurdle for you—or it may not. As one mother admits, "Shyness is not my strong point right now." Either way, you'll want to learn to nurse somewhat discreetly. Practice at home until you can put your baby to the breast without fumbling. When you are ready to nurse outside your home, wear a large, loose T-shirt or blouse to cover you well and give you plenty of room to maneuver; lift

A baby blanket or shawl draped over your shoulder will help you to nurse discreetly in public.

the shirt to nurse, or unbutton it from the bottom. Wearing a sweater or a jacket over your shirt will cover your sides as you lift your shirt up. Or treat yourself to some clothes especially designed for nursing mothers, with buttoned flaps and hidden slits that allow you to nurse both discreetly and fashionably (see "Resources"). For more privacy, a shawl or a baby blanket draped across your shoulder can form a tent over your baby as you nurse.

Wearing your baby in a sling can make discreet nursing infinitely easier. One particularly adept mother found that by nursing her four-week-old in a sling she could keep both her hands free to run the white-elephant booth at her four-year-old's nursery school. Her blouse had a small flap opening for nursing, so she didn't have to pull it up or unbutton it. No one buying a cast-off asparagus steamer or shoe rack ever knew that her baby was doing something other than sleeping.

Try not to feel embarrassed if people notice that you're breastfeeding in public. Nursing openly and proudly reminds people that breasts are first and foremost for feeding babies, and helps our society to become a more welcoming place for mothers and babies.

Right now, of course, your goal is not to change the world, but to return to it along with your baby. Leaving the baby at home while you venture forth might initiate a habit of dividing your life into separate, independent spheres—baby here, work there, while you desperately race back and forth. The result could be utter exhaustion for you and, possibly, a developing distance between you and your baby. Your baby does not want to keep you at home; he simply wants to be with you wherever you go.

Nursing while doing other things at home helps to blend the spheres of your life. When you and your baby are a proficient breastfeeding couple, you may find that you can write letters, work at the computer, or do any number of things while nursing. An ability to nurse while doing desk work or talking on the telephone, in particular, may be key to your success in blending working and mothering in the coming year.

Reconnecting with Your Workplace

If you are taking two to three months off, you may wish to increase communication with your workplace in the second half of your maternity leave. Consider carefully if, when, and how you'll go about this. If you think that talking with your colleagues and perhaps even bringing some work home will make you feel like yourself again, exercise caution. Be certain that you're not hurrying back to work to escape the bewildering demands of your baby. You could end up circumventing motherhood rather than integrating it into your identity—and the result would be a growing distance between you and your child. Focus on becoming in tune with your baby and comfortable in your role as his mother. Perhaps you should consider *extending* rather than shortening your maternity leave (see "Extending Your Maternity Leave.")

If you feel comfortable and confident in your new role as mother, however, reconnecting with work before the end of your maternity leave might benefit you and your baby in the long run. One mother, a sales representative for a publishing company, brought her four-week-old baby into the office to show him off to her colleagues. While there, she casually let her department manager know that she might have time to do some work at home. She left with a stack of paperwork and a mountain of goodwill. Since her baby was settling into a pattern of taking a two-hour morning nap and another in the late afternoon, she managed to get quite a lot of the work done, and, because she hadn't made any promises, she didn't worry about the rest. To show her dedication, she called in a couple of times with questions and comments and even attended a meeting at the office.

Her decision to join the meeting in the sixth week of her maternity leave was especially well considered. She volunteered to come, explaining that her participation would help keep her up to speed while she was on leave. Because all had gone well when she'd brought in the baby for a visit, she brought him along to the meeting as well. "I considered asking permission first," she says, "but I thought they might say no because they'd assume that my baby would disrupt the meeting. I knew he wouldn't and wanted to prove it." She showed up, baby in the sling and notebook in her hand, as if she never imagined his presence would be a problem. If any of her colleagues were surprised, they concealed their reaction. Sitting down at the conference table with her sleeping baby snugly out of sight in the sling, the sales rep turned her attention to the business at hand. The others, taking their cue from her, did the same. When the baby stirred and began to wake at one point, she calmly stood and walked around the room to settle him back to sleep, continuing to participate in the discussion as she did so. The meeting ended shortly thereafter, and she found a private office in which to nurse the baby before heading home.

Asked if she would have nursed the baby, if necessary, during such a meeting, she says, "It depends. If just the people I work closely with were there, I might have nursed discreetly in the room. If others were there with whom I have more formal relationships, and the baby couldn't be satisfied for the time being by sucking on my finger, I might have excused myself to nurse him for five or ten minutes somewhere else—just as someone else might have excused himself to take an important phone call. But I made sure that we nursed just before going to the meeting. I also asked that the meeting be scheduled during the late morning, when I knew he was likely to be sleeping."

This confident, flexible woman demonstrated to her colleagues that she was still a full member of their team without ever camouflaging her new role as a mother. She refused to accept the notion that the mere presence of her baby would diminish her professionalism. Knowing that a fussing, unhappy baby would indeed interrupt the meeting and prevent everyone from getting as much work done as they had planned, she met her baby's needs before they became disruptive demands, while keeping her focus on the meeting. By the end of the meeting all present had revised their attitude about children in the office—and patted themselves on the back for being such an open-minded, progressive company.

Best yet, however, was that when this mother approached her manager about the possibility of working four days a week for the first three months after she returned, her request was granted because she had accomplished so much work during her maternity leave. That four-day week eventually evolved to a five-day week with two of those days spent working at home. Her manager agreed to the latter as a permanent arrangement because he had full confidence that the presence of her child would not stop this employee from getting her work done.

And he was right. She was able to blend her dual roles into one because her work and her mothering did not conflict with each other. Her baby rarely made it impossible for her to work because she made meeting both his physical and emotional needs her first priority—and because she scheduled her work around the times when she knew his needs would be high. Her work rarely disrupted her life as a mother because she refused to stop being a mother while she swam in "professional" waters.

Anyone who has ever attended a La Leche League (LLL) conference has seen many mothers, both lactation professionals and lay leaders, accomplishing the same seamless blending of mothering and other activities. At any regional or national LLL conference, a hundred or more parents spend two to three days in a hotel attending seminars, workshops, and keynote luncheons—just as stockbrokers, computer scientists, and widget salesmen do at their conventions. The big difference is that LLL conventions are also attended by about two hundred children under the age of five. Two- and three-year-olds may run in a circle in the back of a meeting room; a mother with a fussy two-month-old may leave a seminar briefly to comfort her crying baby in the hallway, knowing that someone will catch her up on what she is missing. The adults' tolerance for the children's presence and normal behavior, and their willingness to assist one another, allow them to work productively while meeting their children's needs. And because these needs are met, the children rarely become disruptive.

This doesn't mean that you should launch a campaign to do away with day care and bring everyone's children into your workplace. But neither should you assume that children and work simply do not mix. Consider ways that you might possibly blend work and mothering. If you find yourself immediately dismissing any such possibilities, examine your own assumptions. Bringing your child to work may not be best for either of you, but there may be other ways that you can blend the two sides of your life. The last sections of this chapter may give you some ideas.

Finding Substitute Care for Your Baby

Returning to work will be infinitely easier if you have found someone you trust to care for your baby while you are gone. Unfortunately, day care—and the prospect of searching for it—has become the bogeyman of working parents. The media gleefully tell day-care horror stories without ever mentioning the happy relationships that exist between so many families and their day-care providers. Today day care is considered a modern, Western invention, a dangerous experiment with young lives and family structures.

In fact, day care is nothing new. In most traditional societies, as soon as a child can walk she spends much of her day in a play group of children of mixed ages. She is cared for by a babysitter, usually an older girl who has grown up as a member of the play group herself. Eibl-Eibesfeldt, the ethologist, observes how a child develops in such a setting: The baby watches the group, imitates the older children, and plays simple games with the babysitter. At about age three, the child joins the play directly. "It is in such play groups that children are truly raised," says Eibl-Eibesfeldt.

Group care for children is not only nearly universal in human society, but it offers significant benefits to its participants. The children learn early on that they are a part of a larger community—and they become committed to the well-being of that community right from the beginning. Their social skills are taught and polished by other children, who will be their peer group for life. Each child becomes well-versed in the rich culture of childhood, learning its games and songs and etiquette and bequeathing this culture to children who follow her. As the younger children watch and learn from the older ones, the older ones practice their nurturing skills and begin their climb toward responsible adulthood. Babies are picked up, talked to, cuddled, and played with by children of all ages and by the adults around them. These children develop strong relationships with numerous adults and peers, to everyone's pleasure and benefit.

In our society, unfortunately, day care is not always so safe, loving, and appropriately educational. A baby left from dawn to dusk in a large day-care center with an ever-changing cast of caregivers is not going to benefit from the experience. But when day care is closer to the traditional model, research has shown, children thrive. They receive the social and intellectual stimulation that children have enjoyed through time.

But how, you may wonder, will regular substitute care affect your baby's relationship with you? What if a day-care provider is so wonderful that she and the baby become very close? Can this intimate relationship weaken the maternal-infant bond? Again, research studies (and human history) say no. A child can form a loving attachment to several other adults while maintaining a primary attachment to his mother and father.

A long-term study funded by the National Institute of Child Health and Human Development is following 1,200 children from birth through the first grade to determine the effects of day care on their psychological and cognitive development and physical health. At one, six, and fifteen months, day care appeared to have *no effect* on the children's attachment to their mothers, "regardless of the quality of the care, the age when the child entered it, or the type of care—whether provided by a father, a grandparent, another family or a day care center."

The latest report has a critical caveat, however. It is this: "Child care can make a bad situation worse. If a mother is insensitive to a child's needs, having the child in day care will further weaken the attachment between the two." In other words, even high-quality day care can harm your child's development if your attachment is insecure. Continuing to breastfeed and to draw on the other attachment-promoting tools in your parenting toolbox can help you keep your bond secure—and can help you ensure that day care will play a positive role in your child's life. If you feel that you and your baby are securely attached, that you are in comfortable harmony with each other, then you and your baby are ready for day care.

You and Your Day-Care Provider

Most people who choose child care as a career do so for a combination of reasons. Someone may open a family day-care business so she can stay home with her children. A woman may choose work in a day-care center because she finds nothing so fascinating as the developing minds of young children. Those that stay with their field all have in common a genuine love of children. Professional child care offers too few monetary or social rewards and is much too challenging both mentally and physically for anyone who does not understand and adore children. Enter your search with this thought in mind, rather than with the suspicion and condescension so prevalent now toward child-care providers. Sometimes when we feel new to a situation and unsure of ourselves, we find it difficult to trust others. Take care not to cast your apprehensions about this new stage in your life on every potential provider you meet.

> *"I need to trust my husband, my day-care provider, my parents. I even have to trust my dog to be gentle, for crying out loud. But I can't trust anyone else until I trust myself, which I don't. Of course I trust my husband and my family and the babysitter for all sorts of things, but when I'm not even sure what I expect of myself in caring for Ellie, it's hard to know what to expect of others."*
>
> —WHITNEY SOULE

Review your attitudes: Where do you place paid child care on your personal status ladder? Do you consider a babysitter a valued partner, or do you put her in a class with a housekeeper? Do you prefer to specify all the details of your child's care, or are you willing to let your chosen caregiver employ her experience, wisdom, and understanding of your child? The answers you arrive at will help you decide what kind of child care will work best for you and your family.

Practical considerations will affect your choice of provider. Travel time and difficulty between home, day care, and work must be considered. Would traffic along the route be a daily aggravation? How quickly could you get to your baby in an emergency? Many mothers look for day care near their workplaces so they can drop by in the middle of the day to nurse their babies.

You will also need to consider whether you would like to have your baby cared for in your own home, in a family day-care home, or at a day-care center. Researchers have identified three indicators of quality in any type of day care: the number of children in a group, the amount of time they spend with the same adult, and the investment that the caregiver has made in understanding child development. Evaluate each day-care arrangement according to these basic criteria before examining the details. Also, at every day-care home or center you visit, ask whether parents are allowed to drop in unannounced. If unexpected visits are not welcomed, cross the provider off your list.

FOUR BASIC QUESTIONS FOR DAY-CARE PROVIDERS

- How many children are in a group?
- How much time do the children spend with a particular adult?
- What investment has the caregiver made in understanding child development?
- Are parents allowed to drop in unannounced?

In-Home Care

Hiring a sitter to provide care at home is many people's first choice. It is comforting to know that your baby is being cared for in your own home by someone undistracted by other children. It is wonderfully convenient to have someone arrive in the morning ready to take over when you need to leave for work, even when the baby isn't awake or dressed for the day yet. It means that you don't have to pack a bag or diapers and bottles, bundle the baby up, and deliver her somewhere on the way to work. In addition, this arrangement enables you to oversee every detail of your baby's day more easily. You can decide when your baby should be taken for a walk, when she should be encouraged to take a nap and to have a bottle. You will know exactly what your baby does each day. Another advantage of having your baby cared for in your home is that she won't be exposed to other children's germs and is therefore likely to get sick less often than children in group care. Most important, when she does get sick she can stay home with a familiar caregiver without your having to stay home, too. In-home care may well be the best choice if your baby is just six to eight weeks old when you must go back to work. In this case, you may want to find a babysitter who can come to your home for the first few months, until your baby is older and you feel ready to investigate other possibilities.

Although in-home care seems ideal, in reality it can be problematic. It is extremely expensive. Not only must you pay a full salary, but you must also pay Social Security, Medicare, and federal unemployment taxes for your babysitter, besides filing numerous income-tax forms. If your babysitter requests it, you must withhold federal income tax from her paycheck and file her W-4 forms quarterly. You may need to increase your homeowner's insurance or buy a separate worker's compensation policy in case your babysitter is hurt on the job. Will your babysitter pay for her own health insurance, ask you to pay for it, or go without? How much, if any, paid vacation time will you offer? Will her sick days be paid? You must decide all these things, and keep the necessary records.

Most problems with in-home care, however, have to do with the babysitter's enjoyment of the job and her relationship with her employers. Unless the sitter is a recluse, she may feel too isolated in this sort of job. If she knows other babysitters or mothers in the neighborhood, she can meet them at playgrounds and in backyards to relieve some of the loneliness. But even sitters who manage to socialize this way often move on to other jobs within the first year. All too often, they quit because of an unhappy relationship with the parents.

The fact is someone who excels at child care is likely to value relationships so much that she considers them *to be* her work. Lynn Manfredi/Petitt, a family day-care provider, writes in the journal *Young Children,* "The repetitiveness of chores, delayed gratification of accomplishments, and lack of money seem less important to those who place a priority on relationships. . . . The promise and adventure of authentic, long-term relationships encourage many people to consider spending their days with children for a living" and compensate those who stay in the business. Unfortunately, their special abilities are "virtually invisible; therefore, many people (including caregivers themselves) have difficulty seeing beyond the common assumption that child care providers are paid for doing the chores involved." Many people, Manfredi/Petitt continues, "believe that *just about anyone can do the job* of caring for other people's children. Clearly a new awareness is in order: professional caregiving is a specialized skill based on the ability to love beyond genetic bonds." If you want your caregiver to stay and to be happy in her job, be aware that the quality of your relationship with her is an essential part of her compensation package.

If you have space for someone to live in your home, consider an au pair. Young women and sometimes men are recruited by several established U.S. agencies to live with American families for a year (yes, you would need to find another au pair at the end of the year). Most often from Europe, au pairs come from the Middle East and other parts of the United States as well. Screened and trained before their arrival, au pairs want to learn English, study, and enjoy family life in another culture. For this opportunity (and for approximately $125 per week, plus air fare, room and board, and agency fees—all of which can add up to $5,000 per year), au pairs can provide as much as 45 hours of child care in your home each week. You may instead find your own au pair through family or friends, but you won't have an agency's guarantee that, if things don't work out for one reason or another, you'll have a different au pair within 30 days.

If you want to try an au pair, remember that this person caring for your child will not be a household employee but a temporary member of your family. Remember, too, that most au pairs are in their early twenties, just past their adolescence. Although generally well trained in

> *"Interview an au pair by phone extensively, in her own language if possible. Let each au pair recruit the next one and train her. Most importantly, know that an au pair gives you what you give her. If you treat her as a babysitter, that is what you will get. If you treat her as a member of the family, you will be rewarded with a rich experience, a loving caregiver, and a lifetime friend."*
>
> —A PARENT HOSTING A FIFTH AU PAIR

child care, they may need someone to watch over them. Be prepared to help heal homesickness and a broken heart. Although I hear an occasional disaster story about an au pair, the arrangement is often a delight for everyone involved. A family now hosting their fifth au pair declares, "Choosing the au pair route was one of the best things we ever did. Thanks to that choice, we now have a bilingual (in German and English) four-year-old who can find more countries on a globe than most adults, several extended families in Europe, and a wonderful, lively house."

Another sensible variant on in-home care is shared care. In this arrangement, two (or more) families who live near each other hire someone to take care of their children together. In this way the caregiver makes more money than she would with one child, and the parents pay less than they would for one-on-one care. This arrangement is wonderful for the children, who even as babies enjoy having a buddy to play with every day. The arrangement can also be a lot more fun for the caregiver. Some families alternate the house in which the children and the caregiver stay, by the week or by the month; some use one house exclusively (the host family may pay slightly less than its partner family).

Either way, sharing baby care with another family means building and tending twice as many long-term relationships: Getting along well with the other child's parents is as essential as having a good relationship with the caregiver. The parents need to agree about how they would like the caregiver to handle matters such as naps, meals, and outings. If you would like your baby to have the freedom to explore the house when he begins to crawl, and the other family would like their baby to spend his day securely limited to a playpen, you may run into difficulties.

If you decide that in-home care is the right choice for you, search for the right person along as many avenues as possible. Place a classified ad in your local paper (review the other ads first to inform yourself about going rates and other standards for your area). Write your ad to appeal to the person you have in mind—warm, well-organized, honest. Tell everyone you know that you are looking for a good babysitter; if you find a person recommended by someone you trust, you've struck gold. Put notices up in local colleges and senior centers; lonely retirees can make wonderful substitute grandmothers. If you can afford the fees, consider hiring a nanny through a reputable professional agency.

When you find a prospective caregiver, find out the basics. What is her previous child-care experience? Does she have references? Does she have a valid driver's license? Is she willing to take a tuberculosis test, or has she had one recently? Does she know infant CPR (or is she willing to take a class in it at your expense)? Then ask the essential questions, phrasing them in ways that will not put her on the defensive:

- Why is she interested in this job?
- Does she enjoy child care, or does she perceive it as a job to do until something better comes along?
- Would she be willing to carry your baby in a baby pack or sling, even for much of the day, if the baby is happier that way?
- How does she feel about crying babies? Should they be picked up right away or left to cry?
- How does she feel about breastfeeding, and how does she react to the thought of handling breast milk?

Throughout your interview, keep in mind the most important quality a caregiver should have—the ability to build a loving relationship with your child—and consider all other factors afterward. Look for someone who values relationships and is gifted at forming them. If you and your sitter form a successful match, not only will you avoid having to launch another search in a short while, but most importantly, your baby will benefit from having a consistent, loving substitute caregiver.

Relatives

Substitute care provided by a relative, usually the baby's grandmother or an aunt, can be heaven or a disaster. Some grandparents feel exploited in this role; others wouldn't want their grandchildren to be cared for by anyone else. In traditional societies, of course, caring for children and teaching them cultural lore are primary responsibilities of the elderly. When parents and their parents both favor this form of substitute care, it can serve as the basis of marvelously strong intergenerational ties.

Family Day Care

Family day care can be a wonderful option, too. In most states, a licensed family day-care provider can care for as many as six or, if she has an assistant, ten to twelve children in her own home. The group is usually of mixed ages, typically between a few months and three or four years. This grouping of mixed-age children under the consistent care of one or two adults is much like the way most children have been cared for throughout human history.

Many parents choose family day care primarily because it offers a home environment. The provider's family members may come and go throughout the day. The postman arrives, and the telephone rings. Lunch is in the kitchen, and naps are on beds. Ideally, the provider's home becomes a second home for your child, just as familiar and warm and safe as your own.

Family day-care homes can be found by scanning bulletin boards in libraries, schools, churches, and child-oriented businesses; by reading the newspaper's classified section; and by talking with parents of slightly older children. If your state maintains a registry of licensed day-care providers, obtain a list of all those in your zip code. If you would like to nurse your baby during the work day, ask for a list of providers in the zip code of your workplace as well.

When you interview a prospective day-care provider, try to discern her attitudes about her work, about the children in her care, and about the parents of those children:

- How many years has she been providing family day care?
- Does she take her work seriously, or is it simply a way for her to supplement her family's income without having to leave the house?
- How much does she know—through education, experience, or intuition—about child development?
- Does the provider belong to any professional groups, receive newsletters, or take classes in child development?
- Is she even licensed? (Remember, though, that licensing is no guarantee of excellent care.)
- Does the provider's daily schedule include time outdoors, a midmorning snack, planned activities, and very little or no TV?

When you visit a prospective family day-care home, observe carefully:

- Is it clean and hazard-free?
- Does it have an outdoor play area?
- Where do the children eat and nap?

Observe the provider as she interacts with the children in her care:

- How does she handle a two-year-old who is having a rough day?
- How does she care for a baby at the same time?
- Are the children engaged and happy in their activities?
- Are they comfortable and familiar with the provider?
- Is she positive and warm with them?
- While you and she talk, does she break off the conversation frequently to attend to their needs?

If the answer to the last question is yes, good. This provider has her priorities straight.

As you chat, consider whether you can form a mutually supportive relationship with this provider. Can you learn from her years of experience with children? Will she respect your point of view? Will she be a positive influence in your child's life? You might call the parents with whom the provider now works and ask them to talk about their best and worst experiences with the day-care home.

If you like what you see, talk in depth with the provider about how you feel your baby should be cared for. Tell her you breastfeed, but let her respond before you go further. If she is informed about breastfeeding and supportive, wonderful. If she did not nurse her own children and knows little about breastfeeding, consider whether you'll be able to enlist her support. She must be willing to keep your pumped milk in her freezer and to thaw it for your baby's meals. You must be comfortable nursing your baby in her home. If she would rather not see a mother nurse in her living room, you may need to look elsewhere.

But if you sense that the provider is not disapproving of breastfeeding but simply uninformed on the subject, you might offer her something to read on the importance of breastfeeding and the benefits of breast milk. Nurse discreetly in front of her so she becomes more comfortable with breastfeeding. One mother describes the process of converting her child's caregiver: "I'm the only nursing mother in the five families she works with, and I've nursed longer than any other mother she has known. She knows very little about nursing and expressed breast milk, but I've been slowly making comments and educating her about the differences. It's obvious to me that she probably prefers the ease (for her) of formula, but she is becoming more and more supportive as time goes on." When no supportive day care is available, you may be able to create it.

Once you know you have your provider's support for breastfeeding in general, talk about the details of feeding your baby. Explain that you'd like the bottle feeding of your pumped milk to mimic breastfeeding as much as possible. You would like your baby to be fed in the provider's arms, for example, rather than in a seat with a propped bottle. You would like her fed when she seems hungry rather than on a rigid schedule. Tell the provider, though, that you would prefer she not give the baby a bottle just before you arrive to pick her up, since you'll want her to be eager to nurse (although she probably will be no matter what). Depending on the proximity of the day-care home to your workplace, you may wish to nurse your baby during your lunch hour; if so, ask how the provider feels about this. Talk about solid foods, too, so she knows when and how you would like them to be introduced into your baby's diet. Later you can give the provider detailed instructions on storing, thawing, and feeding breast milk (see page 109).

If your baby is happiest being carried, find out how the provider feels about this. Is she willing to wear the baby in a sling or a baby pack? Wear the baby yourself while visiting with your provider to demonstrate how comfortable and easy it is. Point out how free your hands are, and how content your baby is.

Ask about nap times, too. If one day your baby doesn't seem to want or need her nap, or wants to be held instead of laid down, will the provider accommodate her needs?

When you're sure that you and the provider are compatible, talk with her about practical details—

- How and when does she want to be paid?
- What if you arrive a little late to pick up the baby one day?
- Will you pay if your child is sick and cannot come for a day or two?
- What if the provider gets sick? Does she still get paid?
- Does she collect holiday pay?
- Do you pay when you go on vacation? Does she get paid when she goes on vacation, and when does she go?

An established day-care provider will have ready answers for all these questions. If your chosen provider hasn't set policies, work out mutually agreeable plans ahead of time. Leaving a day-care arrangement that is falling apart because of disagreements and quickly finding a new one tops the list of worst nightmares for working mothers. So be fair as you work out these arrangements. Your day-care provider may want the same paid holidays most employed people receive, or she may set her rates high enough to cover her holidays. She needs vacations, paid or not, more than most people (after all, she lives with her work 24 hours a day). If your child wakes up with chicken pox and can't go to her house, she should still be paid for the day.

Remember that your day-care provider is offering you the most important service possible: help in raising your child. If you have chosen well, the provider will be a ready source of seasoned advice who knows your child nearly as well as you do. Day-care providers often step into the role of the experienced relatives and neighbors who once supplied the parenting wisdom new mothers needed then and still need now. Respect that the provider's work takes place in her own home, where you will always be a guest even though you are paying for her service. Ideally, a family day-care provider is treated with the same sensitivity, affection, and tolerance as the baby's grandparent or aunt. You'll want to let your provider know often how much you appreciate the work she does.

Day-Care Centers

Day-care centers offer both the best and the worst of modern child care. They can be homey, nurturing places with staffs who understand child development and are well trained in caring for children with varying needs. Or they can be impersonal, rigidly organized institutions. You'll know the difference when you see it. The great advantage of day-care centers is their reliability. You can count on a day-care center to be available every day that you must work.

The great disadvantage of using a day-care center is your child's chance of contracting infections there. Finnish researchers have shown that children under two years old in large day-care centers are 36 times more likely than children who stay at home to contract pneumococcal infections (a leading cause of earaches), pneumonia, and meningitis. The risk for children in family day care of catching the same infections is just 4.4 times greater than for those who are cared for in their homes, the Finnish researchers found. Dr. Ben Schwartz, an epidemiologist with the Centers for Disease Control and Prevention, recommends that parents who rely on day-care centers counteract this increased chance of infection by keeping their children away from cigarette smoke, by maintaining good hygiene, and by breastfeeding.

Infant care in a center must be scrutinized with particular care. Sit in a corner of the room for a good half hour or more, and watch how the babies are handled:

- What is the ratio of adults to babies? It should be no more than one to three, with a maximum of eight to ten babies in each group.
- Are the adults holding, rocking, and playing with the babies? Or are the babies tucked into swings and walkers and playpens except when they need to be fed or diapered?
- How consistent is the care? How long have the staff members been at their jobs, and does each take primary responsibility for certain babies? Will there be one person who your baby will recognize as *his* caregiver when you drop him off in the morning?

Ask the same questions of the staff at a center that you would of a family day-care provider. You should be able to find support for breast-feeding at a day-care center. You should be able to drop in at any time to nurse your baby, if you wish. And you should be able to develop close, mutually supportive relationships with the staff members who will be caring for your baby while you work.

Most centers group children by age, combining the two- and three-year-olds in one room and the four- and five-year-olds in another room. Check out these rooms, too, if possible. If you're very lucky, your first day-care arrangement will be your last. If you like this place, you will probably want your child to stay in it at least until preschool and perhaps until kindergarten (some large centers even offer a kindergarten year). What are the older children doing? Are they happily engaged in a variety of projects and imaginative play? Do the teachers sit on the floor to play with the children, and kneel or squat so they can talk with the children face to face? If artwork, posters, and decorations are at your eye level rather than the children's, the center may be more concerned with impressing visiting parents than with enriching the children's days.

Some centers are experimenting with "family groupings," mixing two- to five-year-olds in small groups with one teacher in charge. As in a family day-care home, a neighborhood full of children, or a village, the younger children learn from the older ones, and the older ones enjoy teaching the little ones, learning nurturing skills as they do so. If you find a center with such groupings, observe for a while to see how you like them.

Corporate on-site day-care centers are often touted as the perfect solution to the work-and-family dilemma. American businesses are certainly taking a step in the right direction when they assume a share of the responsibility for helping parents combine work and child raising. Beware, however, of the company-run day-care center that is the pet project of the public-relations department rather than the human-resources department. A mother who works for one large corporation shares her experience: "My company provides on-site day care—if you can ever get in. The waiting list is huge. I put my name on when I was three months pregnant, and my daughter is now four years old. We never got in. This is especially frustrating since the company makes a big deal in the press about its working mother–friendly policy." If you do get your child into an on-site day-care center, there will be the potential problem of having to change centers if you decide to change jobs.

Backup Plans

Whatever child-care arrangement you decide upon, know that the day will come when you need substitute care for your substitute care. Your in-home babysitter gets the flu. Your family day-care provider's mother is having surgery in another state. Your day-care center is closing for three weeks in the summer. Your baby wakes up with a fever and must stay home for the day. What you do in these situations depends very much on your job. Having the flexibility to take the day off or to work at home will make your life infinitely easier. But having backup arrangements will also ease your mind. Do your baby's grandparents live near by? Are they willing to step in in a pinch? How cozy are you with the other parents on your street? Is there an at-home mother who might be willing to be there for you *once in a while* if she knows you'll be there for her on a Saturday night? Bringing your baby to work with you is another possibility not to be casually dismissed. The ins and outs of managing this are discussed in Chapter 6.

Expressing Your Milk

The determination of many mothers to continue breastfeeding and to pump their milk despite obstacles—and the ingenuity they employ in doing so—is inspiring. A postal carrier gave fliers to everybody on her route saying that she was looking for someone to care for her baby while she worked. She easily found a willing mother, and stopped at the woman's house to nurse the baby once while heading out on her route and once on her way back. A sales representative who spent most of each working day on the road bought an electric pump that plugged into the cigarette lighter in her car. "I'd plan to be a little early to each appointment so that I could pump in the car for a few minutes before going in. Pumping actually relaxed me and helped me to prepare myself for each meeting." An ice chest in the back seat kept her milk cool until she reached the babysitter's house at the end of the day.

> *"To nursing moms who are going back to work: It can be done—I have been back for one month and am pumping 16 ounces a day!"*
>
> —A MOTHER, IN AN ON-LINE FORUM

Many mothers choose to pump their milk, storing it for their baby to have while they are apart, simply because they do not want ever to use formula. A full appreciation of the differences between human breast milk and manufactured substitutes makes this reason compelling (reread Chapter 2 if you feel uncommitted to pumping). These mothers know breast milk is the perfect food for their babies' long-term development and health. They know that babies fed only breast milk are sick less often than others—an eminently practical consideration for working mothers.

For other mothers, the choice to pump rather than to use formula is based on emotional reasons. "Pumping my milk helps me to keep my work in perspective and my priorities straight," says one woman. If your goal is to blend the two sides of your life rather than to live them concurrently but separately, pumping can help you to accomplish this.

What if you don't mind feeding formula part time? Can you forego pumping altogether? If you will be working 20 hours or more per week, pumping will probably be essential to establishing your milk supply in the first four months, and very helpful in maintaining it thereafter. Whereas women who supplement with formula have reduced levels of oxytocin, the hormone that causes the milk to let down, in women who feed only their own milk to their babies oxytocin levels actually increase over time, so that they are higher after six months of breastfeeding than after two weeks. And although levels of prolactin, the milk-making hormone, always decline over the period of lactation, they fall faster among mothers who supplement with formula.

In addition, pumping can keep you from becoming uncomfortably full and leaking during the hours you are not with your baby, and can reduce your risk of developing plugged ducts and mastitis.

In a few lines of work, however, pumping simply isn't possible. A police detective writes, "I work surveillance from 9 P.M. to 5 A.M. I'm not alone in the car, and we can't make much noise. Plus, my partner is male. And when I'm not on surveillance, I'm usually in court." But the detective didn't want to wean her baby completely. Having a caregiver feed the baby formula during her work hours, and nursing frequently during her off hours, was the only solution for this mother. Once your milk supply is very well established and your baby is interested in eating solid foods as well as nursing, such an arrangement can work. Breastfeeding does not have to be an all-or-nothing endeavor after the first few months *if* it has been well begun and *if* you nurse freely and frequently during weekends, mornings, evenings, and nights. Sharing a bed with the baby certainly helps.

You may not need to pump your milk at all if you are returning to work part time. If you are working four hours a day or less, you may find that your baby tends to take a long nap while you are gone, and wake up hungry only when you return. "I used to leave a bottle of expressed milk with my sitter," says one mother of a five-and-a-half-month-old, "but my daughter seems to prefer just to sleep and wait for me than drink it." In general, a mother should pump once for every three hours of separation. But your baby's age and nursing pattern, and your susceptibility to plugged ducts, may require you to pump more frequently or allow you to go longer without pumping. If you forego pumping, be sure your baby is draining your breasts at least seven times every 24 hours.

Don't allow the prospect of pumping to make you feel you must choose between weaning your baby and giving up your job. Like breastfeeding, learning to pump is much easier if you go about it calmly and positively. With the new pumps now available, pumping several ounces of milk can be nearly effortless.

Choosing the Right Pump

Today's nursing mothers can choose from a broad range of pumps, from fifteen-dollar drugstore models to the electric-powered machines available for rent. Select a pump depending on how often and where you will need to use it. Will you need to pump only occasionally, or three times a day, five days a week? Will you be pumping in a private office, a parked car, or at home? How much milk will you need to pump? How much time will you have to pump?

Generally, the closer a pump approximates a baby's natural rhythm of 50 to 60 sucks per minute, the better. A pump with a high cycling rate will stimulate more frequent let-downs, withdraw more of your milk, and in these ways help to maintain your milk supply. If you must regularly use a pump with a slow cycling rate, your milk supply may drop to the point where formula feeding becomes essential. Fully automatic pumps are generally the most effective, but they have disadvantages, too—price being the first among them. If you'll need to pump only now and then, you have other good options.

Manual Pumps

If you plan to work no more than three hours a day or mostly at home, you may want to consider a manual pump. Easy to wash and carry, manuals can work well for women who don't want to lug anything that can't be fit into a handbag. Students who already must carry a load of books around often choose manuals because they are small and light and quiet, and do not need an electrical outlet to run (though pumps that run on batteries can also save the search for an outlet). Manuals are also the least expensive pumps available, costing between $15 and $30.

Manuals are more work to use than automatic pumps. You provide the rhythm and the suction by pumping a handle or, with a cylinder pump, by sliding the outer cylinder up and down like a piston. At first you may feel all thumbs; it takes time and practice to learn to use a manual pump. Even after you learn, the repetitive pumping motion can cause muscle fatigue in your forearm. And manual pumping takes concentration; you can't read or daydream while the pump does all the work. Some mothers say that manual pumps require so much effort they can't relax enough to let down their milk, although massaging the breast before pumping really helps. Mothers who are adept with their manual pumps, in fact, often prefer them to all others.

Even if you buy an automatic pump, you may want to get a manual pump as a backup, in case your automatic pump breaks down or there is a power outage. Some automatic pump collection kits can be purchased with an optional attachment for manual pumping.

How you use your manual pump may turn out to be a matter of individual style, something that you will develop only after you've pumped for a week or more. Some mothers prefer to pump in a one-suck-per-second rhythm, like the rhythm of a nursing baby. Others prefer to pump a few times, until the milk lets down, then hold the suction as a spray of milk fills the pump's receptacle. Some lactation consultants warn that because the draw-and-hold method does not mimic a baby's sucking action, it is less effective in maintaining the milk supply than the one-suck-per-second rhythm. Mothers say, however, that drawing and holding is a lot easier on their arm muscles. If you watch your baby nursing, you will see that he begins with a series of short, quick sucks to stimulate your let-down reflex. Then, once he begins to feel your milk flow, he switches to longer, slower sucks, each followed by a swallow. As the flow slackens, he begins sucking with a short, quick rhythm again to stimulate another let-down. Your baby will probably alternate between the two sucking patterns until he is full. The draw-and-hold method is an approximation of this alternating sucking rhythm.

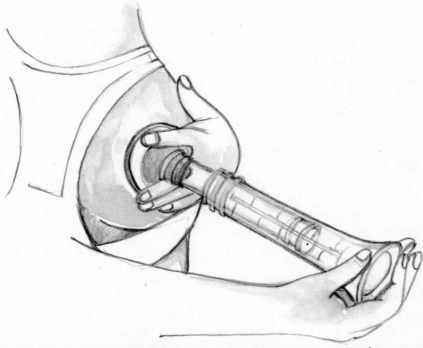

Cylinder pumps may be the most popular of breast pumps. Gently pump the cylinder back and forth until your milk begins to spray into the receptacle.

Cylinder pumps may be the most popular of the manual pumps. Available at most pharmacies and maternity shops, they consist of two piston-like tubes, one inside the other. Sliding one tube up and down while the pump opening (or flange) is pressed against your areola creates the suction and release. Two of the best cylinder pumps are the Comfort Plus (Kaneson) breast pump and an angled-head model made by Ameda/Egnell (see "Resources"). In some models one of the cylinders can be converted into a feeding bottle, but most mothers prefer to pour the milk into a bottle liner or other container for storage, then transfer it to a regular feeding bottle later. (Whether or not the cylinder is designed for feeding, you must pour the milk out when you have more than a couple of ounces to avoid splashing or spilling the milk as you pump.)

The **Ameda/Egnell One-Hand manual breast pump** also works

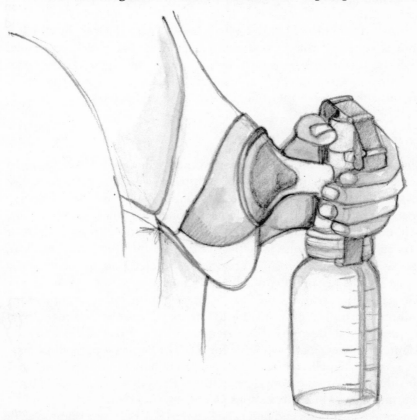

The Ameda/Egnell one-hand manual breast pump requires only one hand to operate and can function as a feeding bottle.

with a piston action. Unlike the cylinder pumps, however, this pump requires only one hand to operate. This frees the other hand for holding a book or nursing the baby on the other breast—an easy way to obtain several ounces of milk in just a few minutes.

Another popular pump is the **Medela SpringExpress.** This pump creates a gentle suction when the plunger is pulled outward; a spring makes the release automatic. The pump can be adapted for use as a milk receptacle with a rental pump.

The Medela and Ameda/Egnell manual pumps share two other advantages. First, the collection vessels really work well as feeding bottles, and are designed so that splash-back and spilling of milk are unlikely. Not having to empty the collection bottle means you won't have to stop and start while pumping. Second, freezer bags can be directly attached to the pump, so your milk can go straight from the pump to the freezer without changing containers and thereby risking contamination.

Avoid any **bicycle horn–style pumps.** These devices, in which a bulb is squeezed for suction, are inexpensive and widely available. Their powerful suck, however, can traumatize the nipple. They collect milk inefficiently, and must be emptied frequently. And since the bulbs are difficult to clean, they may harbor harmful bacteria.

Battery-Operated Pumps

These pumps are most useful for women who work fewer than 20 hours per week. Battery-operated pumps are very portable; some are so small that they can be concealed under a blouse. Most battery-operated pumps are semiautomatic; although they suck automatically, you must push a button or bar to release the suction. In general, most women find these pumps less effective than manual pumps or the more expensive plug-in pumps. Most battery-operated pumps average only 4 to 17 sucks per minute, much less than a baby's 50 to 60 sucks per minute, and so are not good choices for long-term daily pumping or for building the milk supply. In addition, these pumps tend to break down frequently, besides requiring frequent battery replacements. AC adapters, however, are available for most of battery-operated pumps.

Ameda/Egnell, Medela, Evenflo, Marshall Baby Products, and Healthteam all make battery-operated pumps that are available from pharmacies and maternity shops as well as from rental stations run by lactation consultants and La Leche League leaders. These pumps range in price from $30 to $92.

The most expensive pump among them, the **Medela Mini-**

Electric, is fully automatic. It cycles at about 30 to 38 times per minute, slower than the high-end automatic pumps but faster than the other battery-operated pumps. It can be operated with two AA batteries or plugged in.

Some more efficient, fully automatic pumps offer the same convenience and portability of battery-operated pumps (see "High-End Automatic Pumps").

High-End Automatic Pumps

The most popular breast pumps among working mothers are the fully automatic ones. They are ideal for women working more than 20 hours per week. (During an on-line forum discussion on breast pumps, more than fifty mothers praised their automatic pumps, while it was the rare mother who spoke fondly of any other type.) Automatic pumps may enable you to pump easily while reading, talking on the phone, or eating lunch. Their cycling rate most closely corresponds to the sucking action of a baby, so they withdraw milk very efficiently. Best yet, fully automatic pumps offer you the option of double-pumping. Pumping both breasts at the same time can cut in half the time you spend pumping. Lactation consultants report that double-pumping also appears to raise prolactin levels and increase milk production.

The **Medela Lactina Plus,** the **Medela Lactina Select,** and the **Ameda/Egnell Lact-e Lite** electric pumps are the top choices for many mothers. All can be used for single- or double-pumping. Weighing less than five pounds, the Lactina pumps are very portable. Battery packs and adapters for cigarette lighters are available too, so you can pump without being near an electrical outlet. Because the Lactina Select has variable speed control, with this pump you can start slow and build up to 60 cycles per minute, if you prefer. When double-pumping with any of these pumps, mothers report, they can complete a pumping session in eight to ten minutes (allowing them to eat lunch or a snack after rather than during pumping).

The **White River Natural Technologies pump,** also fully automatic, has a soft silicone flange to fit the breast rather than a hard plastic one. With the flexible flange, theoretically, you can combine the sucking action of an electric pump with the breast massage of manual expression. The entire areola and nipple are compressed, just as when a baby breastfeeds. You can use one hand to massage and direct the flange to ensure equal emptying of all parts of your breasts.

You can buy any of these breast pumps, but they cost over six hundred dollars each. Most women who use these pumps rent them. Renting a pump costs $25 to $75 a month, less than the cost of formula. Rental pumps are available from lactation consultants and La Leche League leaders who run pump-rental stations, and from some pharmacies. Call any of the manufacturers (see "Resources") for a list of pump-rental stations near you. In some areas, the White River pump can be delivered to your door for a $10 fee, and picked up whenever you decide. You may wish to try one out for a week or so.

When you rent a pump, you will also need to buy your personal kit of pump attachments; these kits cost between $25 and $45. They contain all the washable tubing, flanges, and bottles that will come in contact with your breasts and milk. Tote bags with cooler compartments are also sold separately.

Medela has recently introduced a sturdy, fully automatic pump intended for sale rather than for rent to nursing mothers. Called the **Pump in Style**, it is said to be as effective as the Lactina Plus. It sells for about $219 as of this writing, through rental stations, catalogs, and baby-supply stores as well as the manufacturer (this is not cheap, of course, but remember that a month's worth of formula costs about one hundred dollars). One of the nice things about this pump is that it

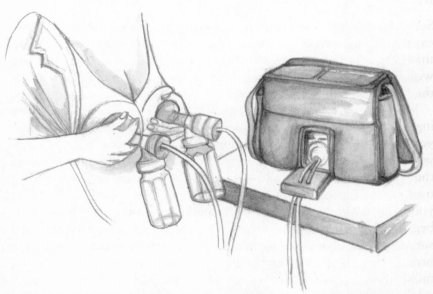

The Medela Lactina Plus and other portable automatic pumps enable you to double pump, thereby obtaining more milk in less time and with less effort than other pumps.

never needs to be removed from its black carrying case (which looks just like a shoulder bag). You simply remove the single- or double-pumping kit and connect their tubes to the front of the bag. Like other fully automatic pumps, the Pump in Style simulates a baby's suck-and-release pattern and can be adjusted for suction strength. The carrier bag includes a cooler compartment with a freezer pack and space for four bottles of milk, as well as ample storage for the pump parts, and even a spot for a photo of your baby. The Pump in Style is guaranteed for 300 hours of operation, or about one year for the full-time worker.

The **Nurture III breast pump**, at about $110, is another pump you can buy rather than rent. Run on electricity from a wall socket, this pump is semi- rather than fully automatic; that is, you control the cycling rate with a finger. The pump also lets you choose among five levels of suction strength, and parts for single- or double-pumping are included. For about $135, you can buy the pump with a tote bag, ice pack, bottles, and a video to show you what to do.

The Pump in Style and Nurture III pumps are available from pump-rental stations, some catalogs and stores, and the manufacturers (see "Resources").

Manual Expression

Some mothers find that they can obtain the most milk when they express it by hand. This is certainly the cheapest option, and the one that requires the least equipment. Before you buy a pump, you may wish to try out hand expressions a few times, perhaps in the shower or the bath or while you are nursing the baby on the other breast.

Begin hand expression by lightly massaging your breasts, relaxing, and thinking about your baby. With a bowl or towel in front of you to catch spraying milk (don't worry about collecting milk yet), cup your breasts with your fingers, your thumb above the nipple. Your thumb and index finger should be about 1½ inches behind the nipple, over the milk sinuses. Draw your thumb and finger outward toward your nipple, gently compressing your breast as you do. As your milk begins to spray, rotate your finger and thumb so that you apply pressure to all the milk sinuses around your nipple. Switch to your other breast when the flow slackens, and then back again to obtain more milk. As you learn to express effectively and to direct the spray accurately, you can begin to collect the milk in a clean container. You may wish to try both breasts at once, although collecting milk can be tricky this way. The Medela Hand-Expression Funnel ($6.95), a lightweight

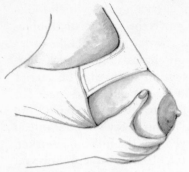

Hand expression takes practice. After massaging your breast, gently compress it with your thumb and forefinger.

Compress the sinuses just behind your nipple and direct the spray of milk into a clean container.

plastic funnel designed to fit into a standard feeding bottle, may help you to hand-express without spills or splashes.

Other Supplies for Expressing Milk

Unless you use a pump that comes with an insulated cooler compartment, like the Pump in Style, you will need something in which to transport your expressed milk. Several coolers designed for the purpose are now available through catalogs, maternity shops, and baby-supply stores. These coolers, which come with freezer packs, will keep as much as 36 ounces of milk cold for up to 16 hours. Some of the coolers double as pump carriers. If you'll be leaving your pump at work or hand-expressing, though, you may want a cooler designed to carry just milk and bottles. A less expensive and perfectly satisfactory alternative is a small picnic cooler or large-mouthed Thermos filled a third of the way with crushed ice. Tuck in a sealed plastic bottle liner full of fresh breast milk, and it will stay well cooled until you are home or at the caregiver's.

If you'll be plugging your pump into a wall socket, you may wish to add a 10- to 12-foot extension cord and a three-prong adapter to your pump carrier, if space allows, so that you'll have more flexibility in where you can pump. Other useful items you might include in your pump tote are extra bottle lids, rubber bands, freezer tape, a hand towel, and a backup manual pump.

Learning to Pump

Wait until your baby is at least two weeks old before trying out your breast pump. Until then, although you may be overflowing with milk and letting down continually (when you're nursing and when you're not), you need to focus on learning to breastfeed your baby rather than on learning to pump. Establishing a bountiful milk supply and becoming comfortable with breastfeeding will promote successful pumping far better than will getting an early start on practice.

You should allow at least two weeks to learn to pump. If you must return to work after just six weeks, begin practicing with your breast pump between two and four weeks after birth. Just be sure to store any of the milk you obtain rather than giving it to your baby. At this age she still needs to breastfeed exclusively to become an expert nurser as well as to keep up your prolactin levels and to establish your milk supply. After the first month has past, you can begin to accustom your baby to a bottle (see "Introducing the Bottle").

If your maternity leave is eight weeks or longer, the fourth or fifth week is an ideal time to take out your pump and familiarize yourself with it. If you are fortunate enough to have a twelve- to sixteen-week maternity leave, you may wish to wait until the eighth week to practice pumping. You will still have a month or more to perfect your technique and build up a substantial supply of frozen milk before your first day of work.

The key to successful pumping is inducing your milk to let down. Until it does, you may be lucky to collect even an ounce of the thin milk stored in your ducts. Once your milk lets down, though, the pump's collection bottle may fill fast, especially if you're pumping in the early morning.

Relaxation promotes a speedy let-down even with a less effective pump. Begin any pumping session with a routine that will help you relax and feel comfortable. A good time to pump is the early morning, when your milk supply is most plentiful and you are probably more relaxed than at the end of the day. Pump soon after feeding your baby. (If your baby has taken only one breast at the last feeding, you should be able to collect enough milk to store.) If you are using a pump that requires only one hand, you can pump while simultaneously nursing your baby; your milk will let down very quickly this way.

First drink a glass of water, and wash your hands. Choose a comfortable chair near a table where you can set your pump and bottles. Set up the pump following the manufacturer's instructions. Expose both your breasts (you'll learn to pump with less exposure

Gerry Anne's Recipe for Pumping Success

(From Gerry Anne Dubis, a La Leche leader)

♦ *Before beginning your pumping career, it is important to understand two things:*

1. Morning pumpings will yield the most milk, whether you're pumping at home or at work.
2. The amount of milk yielded when you pump regularly during the day will decline as the day goes on. This is normal for most women.

♦ *Begin to pump this way:*

1. Nurse the baby well on one side between 5 A.M. and 8 A.M. in the morning. Pump the other side for approximately 10 minutes. Then nurse the baby on the pumped side to further drain the breast.
2. Refrigerate or freeze the milk.
3. Later in the morning, about one and a half hours after a feeding or during the baby's nap, pump both breasts.
4. Chill this milk, add it to the milk already refrigerated, and then freeze the container. If you froze the milk you collected earlier, freeze this portion separately, or chill it before adding it to the frozen milk. (Do not add warm milk to chilled or frozen milk.)
5. You have finished pumping for the day. For the rest of the day, just take care of yourself and your baby.

♦ *Assuming you collect 3 to 4 ounces of milk per day, pumping twice a day for three weeks will put 63 to 84 ounces of milk in your freezer before you return to work. With practice, you may soon be able to pump as much as 8 ounces in a day. At that rate, in three weeks you can collect 164 ounces!*

later). Lightly massage your breasts with your fingertips in small circular patterns to stimulate your let-down reflex. Holding a warm (not hot) heating pad against your breasts can help, too. Looking at your baby, imagining her, or sniffing a piece of clothing she has worn recently may also speed the let-down of your milk.

Bring the flange of the pump against your breast so that your nipple is centered in the opening. (If you have very large nipples and are using an electric pump, you can buy a special flange from the pump manufacturer. Ask a lactation consultant or the woman who runs your rental station about this.) You may wish to dampen the flange to create a stronger seal between it and your breast. Turn an automatic pump to its lowest setting, or begin to manually pump in a slow, gentle rhythm. Gradually increase the speed.

Limit your pumping sessions to 5 minutes per side until you feel comfortable with the process, then increase your pumping time to 10 minutes per breast. Since pumps exert considerable suction on the nipple, you should go slow until you're accustomed to the suction, know how to control it, and can avoid getting sore or even injuring your nipple.

With practice, you should be able to drain your breast in 10 to 15 minutes if you're using a fully automatic pump, 20 to 30 minutes otherwise. In general, pumping should take only as long as it takes to nurse your baby.

Save any milk you collect (see "Storing Milk"). Every 2 to 3 ounces is another bag of gold in your freezer. To increase your stock of frozen milk, you might grab your pump after any feeding when the baby has taken only one breast.

Another trick for maximizing your milk collecting, if you are using a single-side pump, is to switch back and forth between your breasts every four minutes or so. Double-pumping—pumping both sides at once—is even more effective in increasing milk output.

If you find, after several attempts at pumping, that your pump isn't generating a full let-down, or that your breasts are still heavy with milk after pumping, consider getting a new pump with a higher cycling rate. If you're already using an automatic pump with a high cycling rate, get a double-pump kit, and pump both breasts at once.

Storing Milk

In the months to come, your baby's appetite and your milk production may not always match up perfectly. During growth spurts he may want to eat more than you are producing. It is for these times that you are pumping and freezing your milk now. When you are back at work, you'll leave the fresh milk you pump each day with the baby's caregiver, who will feed it to the baby the following day. You may never need most of the milk in your freezer. You will be glad you have it, though, when your baby's appetite increases beyond your production. And your frozen milk will be indispensable if you must take a trip without your baby or find one day that you have no chance to pump. Some days you'll produce more milk than your baby wants, and on these days you can augment your frozen supply.

Breast milk is a remarkably stable fluid. Fresh breast milk contains elements that keep bacteria from growing in it for several hours after it's been expressed. (Manufactured formula, in comparison, is an unstable substance that spoils quickly.) One study found no significant difference between the bacterial levels in milk stored for 10 hours at room temperature and milk refrigerated for 10 hours.

MAXIMUM TIMES FOR STORING BREAST MILK

Fresh Milk
At room temperature: 6 hours
Refrigerated: 5 days

Frozen Milk
In a freezer compartment inside a refrigerator: 2 weeks
In the freezer of a refrigerator-freezer with separate doors: 2 months
At a constant 0 degrees Fahrenheit: 3 months
Thawed in the refrigerator: 24 hours (do not refreeze)

Still, you should handle your milk with care. Don't store it in the door of your freezer; the temperature there fluctuates a lot when the freezer is opened and closed. Store your milk in the back of the freezer, where the temperature is constant. Do not refreeze thawed milk.

Most mothers use plastic bottle liners or plastic food storage containers for storing their breast milk. Mothers who pump a lot generally prefer plastic bottle liners, and keep a supply of both 4- and 8-ounce liners on hand. Because glass containers best preserve the protective white cells in milk, and because 60 percent of secretory IgA (one of the most valuable elements in breast milk) sticks to plastic, hospitals use glass bottles to store breast milk for premature babies. But plastic containers are lighter and less breakable, and therefore more convenient to transport and store than glass bottles. Besides, if your baby is a healthy-full-term infant, losing a small measure of the leukocytes or secretory IgA in two or three feedings a day should not make a real difference. However, plastic can change the taste of milk that has been stored in it for a while. If your baby seems to be balking at the taste of your thawed milk, you might try switching to glass bottles.

Several companies make bags designed specifically for storing frozen breast milk. Ameda/Egnell, Medela, Kaneson, and the Breast-feeding Support Network all produce milk bags that are heavier than bottle liners and less likely to split open when your milk expands in freezing. Depending on the type of pump you use, you may be able to pump your milk directly into freezer bags, thus saving valuable time at work. Also, all of these bags have labels on which you can write the date without risk that the ink might leach into the milk (because of this risk, lactation consultants recommend against writing directly on the plastic). Milk storage bags range in price from 22 to 43 cents per bag.

Except for milk storage bags and bottle liners, which come sterile in the box, any glass or plastic container to be used for storing breast milk should be washed in hot, soapy water.

Freeze small amounts of milk at a time—1 to 3 ounces in 4-ounce bags, or 4 to 6 ounces in 8-ounce bags. Never fill a bag to the brim, because milk expands when it freezes. You will need a little extra room besides if you're going to roll down the top of the bag to seal it. If you use disposable bottle liners, double-bag your milk before freezing it to prevent leaks.

Before you seal a bag, carefully squeeze out the air at the top. Then roll the bag down to about an inch above the milk, and seal it with a bit of freezer tape. Or twist the top of the bag, bend the top down, and seal the bag with a rubber band or a wire twist tie; it will be easier to open this way. Write the date on the tape that seals the bag, on a separate piece of tape, or on the label provided for this purpose. To keep your milk bags from getting jostled or buried in the freezer, you might place them upright in a heavy plastic container.

If you add fresh milk to a container partly filled with frozen milk, be sure to cool the fresh milk in the refrigerator before you do so.

Using Frozen Milk

Always use your oldest milk first. Keep a few bags of milk in your caregiver's freezer so she'll have it when she needs it.

When you want to use frozen milk, thaw it by holding the container under warm, running water, or rest the container in a bowl full of warm water. Never boil breast milk, and never microwave your milk; either treatment would destroy the milk's immunological properties, making it less stable and less healthful for your baby. Also, microwaving could cause hot spots in the milk that might burn your baby's mouth.

Before feeding the thawed milk to your baby, shake the bottle to mix in the cream.

If you would like to give your baby an especially filling, high-calorie meal, you can create a double-cream feeding from your pumped supplies. When you store your milk in a transparent container, you will see that the milk separates, with the cream rising to the top. After thawing the milk from two containers, pour off the cream from both, and combine them in a third container, leaving the skim milk for another feeding. The extra-rich feeding may keep your baby satiated for a good part of the time while you are at work, or can help tide her through a growth spurt while your milk supply is catching up. The skim milk may be useful another time, such as at the end of a work day when your baby wants to nurse but you have not yet arrived to pick her up. The skim milk will satisfy her for a while, but she should still have enough appetite to nurse long and well when you arrive.

Introducing the Bottle

If your baby is adept at breastfeeding and you feel confident in your milk supply, you can introduce the bottle in the third week after birth. Before this point your baby may still be learning to nurse at the breast. Switching back and forth between breast and bottle can confuse a young baby, since artificial nipples require an entirely different sort of sucking pattern. Whereas in breastfeeding a baby needs to stimulate a let-down and draw the milk out, milk flows out of bottles without much effort on the baby's part at all. If you introduce the bottle too early, then, your baby may become frustrated at the breast and soon reluctant to nurse at all. Do allow at least ten days for your baby to learn to drink from the bottle.

If you have a three- or four-month maternity leave, you may want to postpone introducing the bottle. Keep in mind, though, that babies who first try the bottle after two months of age are often intractable in their preference for the breast. There are ways around a baby's refusal, but it may be easier to avoid the problem by introducing the bottle sooner, and offering it once or twice a week thereafter to keep it familiar to him.

Give your baby expressed breast milk for these feedings, even if you have decided to use formula instead of pumping at work. Breast milk and formula do not taste the same; try them and see for yourself. You will want to introduce one new thing at a time, first an artificial nipple and later a new taste.

Your baby is much more likely to accept a bottle from someone other than you. Ask your mate, your babysitter, or a friend to offer your baby a bottle of milk once a day, preferably at about the time your baby will need a bottle when you are at work, and in a place other than the one where you usually nurse. Your baby should not be very hungry when offered a bottle for the first time; try these first feedings about one hour to one and a half hours after nursing. Ask your helper to hold your baby much as you do when nursing, and then to tickle his lips with the nipple and dribble a little milk into his mouth, just as you might have done when first coaxing him to nurse.

You may want to go for a walk during these initial bottle feedings, since if your baby can hear or smell you he may refuse the bottle without trying it (however, some parents report success with wrapping the baby in his mother's blouse or nightgown while offering the bottle).

If your baby refuses the bottle at first, this does not mean he will never accept it. Have your helper keep trying—calmly, gently, and without any force whatsoever—for about 10 minutes. Then your helper should stop until the next day.

Once your baby is taking the bottle, your helper or another person should give him a bottle once or twice a week to keep him used to it until you go back to work. (From the day you start work until weaning, however, follow the nursing-working mother's rule: "My baby gets a bottle when I'm not there, and breastfeeds when I am there.")

What do you do if your baby is steadfast in his refusal to bottle-feed? There are numerous ways to help him adjust to an artificial nipple. There are even several ways to feed him without using a bottle at all. Above all, however, don't panic. His rejection of the bottle does not mean you cannot return to work.

If your baby is older than eight weeks and is handling and mouthing teething rings and other toys, you may wish to add a plastic bottle with a nipple to his toy collection. He will naturally explore it with his mouth. At some point you may wish to put an ounce of breast milk in the bottle and see what happens. Some babies prefer a warm, soft nipple (sound familiar?). Warm the bottle nipple under warm running tap water before offering it. If your baby is teething, though, you might try cooling the bottle nipple in the refrigerator to soothe his gums. Try different types of bottle nipples to find a shape or texture your baby will accept. Sometimes a nipple made out of silicone is accepted when a rubber one is not. Some babies prefer a larger or smaller nipple hole.

**HOW TO PREPARE FOR YOUR RETURN TO WORK:
TWO TO FOUR WEEKS AHEAD**

- Visit your workplace with your baby, but think carefully before bringing work home.
- Select a child-care provider, and talk with her about breast-feeding.
- Make a backup child-care plan.
- Get a good pump, and learn to use it.
- Teach your baby to take a bottle.

Ask your helper to try different feeding positions and settings. Holding the baby facing outward while walking often works wonders. Some babies will take a bottle while being swayed from side to side. Some babies who refuse a bottle at other times will take a bottle when they are riding in a carseat. Once a baby becomes accustomed to taking a bottle in one place he is more likely to drink from it in other places.

Some babies will take a bottle from their caregivers at day care when they won't from anybody at home. These babies seem to be thinking, "I'm not at home, so I don't eat the way I do at home." Of course, many caregivers have years of experience helping babies to feel at ease in new situations.

If you've tried all possible nipples, positions, and combinations of the two without success, you can forgo bottles altogether. One mother says that her baby took a bottle "only a couple of times, when hunger won out. We eventually gave up trying, and he soon drank from a cup, anyway." If your baby is four or five months old when you return to work, you may prefer that he be fed from a cup; this way you won't have to wean him from a bottle later. Some mothers have used their babies' refusal to take a bottle as a reason to stay home until their

A baby who is reluctant to take a bottle may accept one when held facing outward.

babies have reached at least four months old and can drink from a cup. This isn't necessary, though; babies as young as eight weeks can be fed from a cup. Medela and Ameda/Egnell make soft feeding cups intended as an alternative to bottles for young babies. Babies have also been successfully fed with spoons and eyedroppers.

Preparing Your Home and Family

About two weeks before your first day back at work, you may wish to take a few other steps to ensure that the transition causes you as little stress as possible. Expect the first weeks back at work to have much in common with the first weeks of motherhood. Small events will loom large. Fatigue will be a familiar companion as you learn to manage both work and mothering. For now, prepare your home much as you may have done in the week before your baby was born. Cook several main dishes, and freeze them. Stock up on nutritious foods that can be prepared quickly. Consider asking a friend or relative to help out. A woman whose mother came to help when her baby was born asked her mother-in-law to come for her first week back at work. Just as you did after giving birth, you will need both emotional support and physical assistance with household and child-care chores, and as much rest as possible.

Your mate can make all the difference during this transition period. If he truly bears at least 50 percent of the household duties, you are already a long way toward meeting the challenge of working and mothering. Unfortunately, many husbands may support their wives' return to work and say they'll help out, but don't really comprehend what needs to be done. As Arlie Hochschild's groundbreaking book *The Second Shift* documents, in only 20 percent of dual-career marriages do men share housework equally with their wives. While the women in this study revealed over and over again that they accept this inequity to keep the peace, they tend to suffer with chronic exhaustion, low sex drive, and frequent illness.

Talk with your spouse as frankly as you can about how the two of you will manage household tasks. Be clear about the difference between helping out and taking full responsibility. Does cooking dinner mean just that, or does it include the planning, shopping, and cleanup? Does getting the dry cleaning done mean dropping the clothes off at the cleaners on the way to work, or does it mean collecting the clothes each week, bringing them in with instructions for special treatment, keeping track of the receipt, and picking them up on time (all without being reminded)? In many marriages in which the husband comfortably takes credit for half the domestic tasks, neither he nor his wife acknowledges the weight of the details surrounding each task that is performed by the wife. Going back to work does not mean that everything is back to normal and that you are ready to do everything you did before. In your first six months back at work, as in your first days at home with your baby, you will need to focus on caring for yourself and your baby during all your off hours. Your mate can make this possible.

If you are single, you'll need to rely on your network of friends and relatives during the next six months. Do you have an especially supportive and close friend who can help out for a while? You'll need to mother yourself as well as your baby, not pressure yourself to "just get through it." Do only absolutely necessary tasks, and praise yourself lavishly—you deserve it.

In these last two weeks before you go back to work, arrange several visits with your baby's caregiver to increase everybody's familiarity and comfort with one another. On one of these visits, leave your baby with the caregiver for an hour or two while you do a few errands. If your baby will be staying in another home or in a day-care center, take a "dry run" day in the last week: Get up, pump, dress, and take your baby to day care as if you were going to work. You don't need to leave the baby there all day, but going through the morning routine will build your confidence. You might want to spend half a day at the caregiver's home or at the day-care center with your baby as the caregiver carries on with her normal routine. Then you'll have a clear picture in your mind of what your baby's days will be like when you're not there.

Plan your working wardrobe with pumping in mind: separates with front-buttoning blouses will be easiest, and light colors and prints will best camouflage leaks. Your old business wardrobe may not fit as well as it once did (yet). Sort through it to see what is still useful and what needs to be set aside for a few more months. Buy something new that will make you feel attractive, confident, and comfortable on your first day.

In a quiet moment, visualize yourself back at work, and feeling good about it. Remember the moments that you've most enjoyed in your job and the people with whom you work well. Remember the satisfaction that you have received from doing challenging work well. You may feel now as though you are standing on the edge of a precipice about to jump into a dark chasm. The moments before the leap may be more frightening than the leap itself. Draw on the lessons you've learned in these first months of motherhood; trust yourself to be flexible and capable enough to handle problems as they come up. Take one day at a time. The first weeks back at work will pass quickly; you and your baby will soon settle into a new routine that includes your job.

Preparing Your Workplace

The first few weeks of working full time while mothering a new baby can be traumatic. Easing back into the old routine gradually means less stress for mothers and babies—and less risk to the company of having to hire and train someone new when a burnt-out mother decides to quit. For this reason many large companies, including Aetna Life and Casualty Company, AT&T, Chase Manhattan Bank, IBM, and Patagonia, have institute "phase-back" policies to allow new mothers to return to the workplace gradually. Talk with your manager or staff about your plans for your first weeks back at work. You might see if you can arrange to work four-day weeks, taking Wednesdays off, for the first month or so. A gradual return to work can minimize your stress and fatigue, which could affect your milk supply and lead to plugged ducts and even mastitis. If you must work full time from the beginning, ask if you can start on a Thursday or a Friday so that your first day or two will be followed by a weekend in which you can recuperate.

HOW TO PREPARE FOR YOUR RETURN TO WORK: THE LAST TWO WEEKS

- Arrange a short first work week
- Enlist support from your mate and from friends or relatives
- Find a place to pump
- Select clothes you can nurse in
- Do a "dry run" to day care

If you don't have a private office and aren't sure where else you can pump, stop by your workplace "just to say hello," and scout out a good pumping place. You might ask an understanding coworker who has an office if you can borrow it briefly twice a day. Conference rooms, storage rooms, and nurse's offices have all been used by nursing moms. Bathrooms are sometimes a necessary though unfortunate last resort. Some mothers don't mind pumping in bathrooms; most, however, intensely dislike doing so and can't relax when they try. An acceptable bathroom must be private and clean, with a small table, a place to sit other than the toilet, and an electrical outlet (keep an eye out for covered electrical outlets that can be uncovered if you so request). Don't let someone bully you into using the bathroom, however, because he or she equates breast milk with other bodily fluids. You are preparing a meal for your baby, and deserve an appropriate place in which to do so. Some mothers have found that the best place for pumping is their own car in the company parking lot. With a sunshade across the front and a towel or two draped across the windows, your car can be private and, because it is your *own* place, relaxing.

If no suitable pumping place is available, consider proposing to your company that one be created. Talking to your company about special arrangements to satisfy your needs as a mother can be tricky. You want to avoid setting off alarm bells about your commitment to your job without giving into pressures to hide your motherhood. How you'll make your request for space and time to pump your milk depends very much on the culture of your company—and on your own feelings about your rights as a mother. You probably need 15 to 30 minutes twice a day to pump your milk and a clean, private place in which to do it. (If your baby is in day care nearby, you may want 30 minutes twice a day to stop in and nurse.) These requirements may last from three months to a year. The accommodations you're asking for will make a great deal of difference to you and your baby and very little difference, in the end, to your employer.

Medela, a breast-pump manufacturer, developed a program in 1992 to assist nursing mothers with these matters. The Sanvita Corporate Lactation Program provides breastfeeding information to managers and nursing employees and assists in setting up private and pleasant places in which mother can pump. Medela will even assign a lactation consultant to manage the pumping station and counsel the mothers who use it. See "Resources" for more information on the Sanvita program, and for a sample letter requesting a pumping station and outlining the benefits to businesses of supporting breastfeeding mothers.

Extending Your Maternity Leave

According to the Pregnancy Disability Act and the Family Medical Leave Act, you have a right to six weeks of maternity leave with disability pay plus six more weeks without pay—*if* your employer has 50 or more employees, and *if* you have worked for that employer at least 25 hours per week for the year preceding your leave. If your employer offers only these minimum maternity benefits (or if you're ineligible even for these), and you want to extend your leave to, say, four months, you have some negotiating to do. Your success will depend on how valuable you are to your employer and how flexible company policies are. Consider enlisting your doctor's support to drive home the importance of establishing a close attachment to your baby through full-time breastfeeding before returning to work. Come armed with the names of comparable companies that allow longer leaves.

Alternative Work Arrangements

No matter how long your maternity leave, when it's over you may not feel ready to put your baby in day care from dawn to dusk five days a week. Consider whether one of these innovative arrangements might be the solution:

First, you might ask your employer for a flexible schedule. "**Flextime**" has become a standard at many companies, thanks to the requests of desperate and determined parents. Usually, employees can start and finish work when they prefer, as long as they are on the job during core working hours, such as 10 A.M. to 3 P.M. If both parents are lucky enough to work on flextime schedules, one can leave for work early and come home early, while the other leaves later and comes home later, so the baby need spend only five or six hours in day care.

Compressed work weeks for full-time employees are also gaining in popularity; you might work four 10-hour days followed by three days off, or three 12-hour days followed by four days off. Although such a schedule may sound appealing, it wouldn't necessarily work out well. Your work days would be long and tiring, and your days off might also have a wearying intensity as you try to make up for lost time with your child. You would need to pump at least three and probably four times each work day. Compressed work weeks divide a person's life cleanly in two, with work and home hardly mixing at all. Many people feel very comfortable with this and prefer it to the usual schedule, but consider carefully how stressful you would find the weekly transitions before suggesting a compressed work week to your employer.

Telecommuting may be a nearly ideal solution for combining work and mothering. Thanks to computers, modems, faxes, e-mail, voice-mail, and call-forwarding, you can be in contact with your co-workers almost as easily as if you were at work. One woman describes her situation: "My boss was wonderful to let me work at home for the last two months of a difficult pregnancy. I still work at home now several times a week, but in order to manage it with my boss, I provide her with a weekly report of what I've accomplished. I also check voice-mail and e-mail messages several times a day. We periodically go over goals and achievement to make sure it works well. I still have to put my kids in day care when I'm home, but the benefit is that I can pick them up when I'm done with my work—usually around 2:30—rather than at the end of the work day and a long commute."

Telecommuting arrangements can be a boon to business as well. At one Aetna Health Plans office, telecommuting has increased the productivity of the claims processors by 29 percent. Workers are also making fewer errors, and the company is saving twelve thousand dollars on office space.

Although working at home would allow you more time with your baby, you might miss the casual interaction with your colleagues—and they might eventually decide that they really do need you in person. Anther woman recalls, "I worked out of my home for six months after my son was born, via computer, fax, and phone. When I suggested extending the arrangement, my company said they preferred to see my face full time. It comes down to their being able to pop their heads into my office with a simple question." Telecommuting may work well enough, however, until your baby is older and you feel more comfortable being separated.

Part-time work may be a solution for you, if you can afford it. Although your income would decrease, so would your day-care expenses. Is there a part of your job that you do especially well and for which your employer most values you? Write a proposal redesigning your job into a part-time position dedicated to that function, with prorated pay and benefits. Be sure to negotiate an hourly rate, so that if you put in extra hours you'll get paid for them. You might propose that you work an average of 20 hours a week, with an annual maximum of 1,000 hours, so that your schedule can fluctuate to meet the needs of your workplace and your family.

If your employer agrees to a part-time schedule, be prepared for changes in the way your colleagues and managers perceive you. You may find that you are not taken as seriously as you were before, or that you've lost some of the perks that went with your previous position, such as the parking place or the private telephone line. You may find you can't advance as a part-timer. One manager for a large insurance company writes, "In my experience, part-time employees are often treated like second-class citizens. The men in management tend to think their heart is no longer in their career. I'm treated as if I no longer want to be in the fast track or considered for promotion. I am someone who moved up rapidly, but the corporate culture still makes me feel this way."

Sitting on a plateau for a few years, however, won't necessarily keep you from eventually reaching career heights. A government lawyer has no regrets about her choice to work part time while her children were babies: "When my children were five and three, I returned to work full time and have since been promoted twice. My children have always been well cared for, and I have a husband who believes that he is as responsible for their care as I am. I am very happy with the choices I made and continue to make. Promotion may take longer, and people in the workplace need to be convinced that you really care, but it is possible." If there is ever a time in your life when you might want to ease your career's trajectory a bit while still keeping your foot in the door, now is probably it.

Job sharing is a part-time work arrangement that often makes sense for both employer and employee. In this arrangement, two employees manage the responsibilities of one position. Often one person works Monday through Wednesday and the other Wednesday through Friday; they catch up with each other midweek. The employer benefits from having two energetic employees, and all the experience and resources they both bring to the job, for the price of one overextended employee. The employees divide the benefits and the salary in a way that works for them and their firm. Ideally, the job-sharing partners are flexible enough to step in for each other when one misses work because of a sick child or vacation.

To pursue any of these arrangements, your first step is to write a confident, convincing proposal for your employer. Describe the arrangement you desire, its benefits to your employer, and how you would handle situations that might arise. You might first read *Breaking Out of 9 to 5: Making Your Dream of Escaping the Rigid 9-to-5 Workweek Come True,* by Maria Laqueur and Donna Dickinson. It covers everything you need to know to arrange your job to fit your life.

Staying Home Instead

What if you are about to go back to work but every cell in your body is screaming that this is not what you want to do? And yet the alternative, quitting and staying at home full time, just doesn't seem workable? There's the loss of income, for starters. If you're like most women these days, the money you make probably goes to the mortgage or the rent, groceries, college savings, and other necessities. You may also be uncomfortable with the idea of walking away from your career and your life outside the home. Who will you be without your professional identity? Will your mind turn to mush? Will you go stir-crazy? What will you do when your children are no longer small?

These are all good questions, although they show a lack of appreciation for the creative pleasures and intellectual demands of mothering. Mothers who have made the decision to stay home after years of working in jobs they enjoyed say that many of the assumptions made about staying at home just aren't true. Listen to one: "As someone who had always worked, I struggled with the decision of whether to quit. I eased out of it. At first, I gave up my management position for a part-time position with the same company. (In other words, they thought a part-timer couldn't handle that much responsibility.) But as my second child came along and my first went into kindergarten, I knew I had to try the stay-at-home thing. It has been wonderful, and it's true, even if the kids are playing while you're doing chores, they are just enjoying being in their own environment with their own stuff and you in the background. It is a major security thing for them. At least that's how I've found it. No regrets so far. I also worried that I would be bored, bored, bored, but, just like the kids, I'm not. Quite the opposite. One thing to remember is, if you quit, it's not permanent, you can always go back. Give yourself the opportunity to make an informed decision."

Life is long, and childhood is brief. If you step out of your career path for a few years, you can step back into it later and perhaps follow new directions that you hadn't considered before. That's not to say that the progress of your career won't be altered by leaving it for a few years. Your field will evolve, and the colleagues you have left behind will advance during your absence. But in a decade or so, they may be burned out and thinking about a change, while you will be hitting your prime with a maturity earned through motherhood. To keep from feeling adrift, you might design a 10-year plan. What would you like to be doing in 10 years, when your child is on the verge of adolescence? How can you prepare for that goal, year by year, as he grows?

And what about the financial issues? There may be more leeway here than you imagine. First of all, you might consider turning some of your specialized skills into a freelance or consulting business. As corporations "downsize," they increasingly rely on outsiders to provide services formerly done by staff members. Editors, writers, public-relations specialists, designers, accountants, and computer experts are just a few of the professionals who have found a demand for their independent services. Your own company may jump at the chance to employ your expertise without having to pay the overhead costs of office space, insurance, and other benefits. You will lose those benefits, of course, but if your spouse's job pays for health care and has retirement benefits, perhaps for a few years you can manage. Flexibility and time at home with your child is your compensation package now.

ON YOUR OWN: FREELANCE BUSINESSES IN DEMAND

Desktop publishing, graphic design, illustration, photography, indexing, technical writing, journalism, editing, website management, on-line computer businesses, computer programming, computer illustration and design, résumé preparation, medical transcription, legal services, public-relations consulting, sales, tax-form preparation, accounting, financial planning, mortgage brokering, property management, architecture and building design, interior decorating, catering, massage, pet care, cleaning, tutoring, day care, nursery or greenhouse operation, "reassurance" services for the elderly and house-bound, postpartum care, labor support, childbirth education, managing book and software fairs at schools, educational counseling, CPR and first-aid teaching, crafts, landscape architecture and garden design, environmental management consulting—and more!

Equate cutting back expenses with earning income; every dollar you save is indeed a dollar earned. Begin with your current salary. Now add up all the costs of working, including day care, clothes, commuting costs, and taxes, and subtract them. Take the sum that is left, and subtract the cost of everything you now spend money on that you can possibly do without. (Do take into account the expected and unexpected costs of having a child, from life insurance to emergency room visits.) What remains? Is it an amount that you can earn in various ways without relying on a full-time job? Is it an amount you and your family can manage without for a few years? Numerous books are full of clever ideas for reducing expenses. Take a look at *Staying Home Instead: Alternatives to the Two-Paycheck Family,* by Christine Davidson, and *The Tightwad's Gazette,* a monthly newsletter. As one mother writes, "If you really want to stay home, find a way. I was certain we could never afford it, as my paycheck paid more than half of the mortgage, but it is amazing what you can do!"

No one of the work options described here is right for everyone. Design your life in a way that is right for you. And remember, whatever your choice, if you're happy, your baby will be happy, too.

CHAPTER SIX

YOUR RETURN TO THE OUTSIDE WORLD

*"Everybody expects me to be the same
person. But I'm a different person."*

YOUR FIRST DAYS BACK at work can feel like a visit to a distant planet. You speak the language, and the inhabitants appear to recognize you, but you feel very far from home. Give yourself time; the strangeness will fade.

Although these first weeks will pass quickly, they can be physically and emotionally draining. You may feel just as spent and fragile as you did in the first weeks after the baby was born, but now you must be on your feet and doing things all day. Your emotions may be as strong as during those newborn days—and taxing your energy reserves as much as any physical demands. Not only are you adjusting to being separated from your baby for hours at a time, but your old life and your new life stand face to face—and you must find a way to blend them into one. On top of these challenges, when you go back to work other people assume that everything is back to "normal," and that you are ready to carry on in all ways just as you did before the baby was born. You may be making that assumption yourself.

Now as in the newborn days, you need to take especially good care of yourself. Now as then, you need to reach out to your sources of support. Phone working friends with babies for encouragement, and talk with colleagues who have tread this path. Consider asking a helpful relative, if you haven't already, to stay with you now for a week or more. Accept offers of assistance from friends and neighbors (although such offers may not be as plentiful as just after the birth). Be sure that your mate, especially, does not assume that the end of your maternity leave means that now everything is (at last) as it was before. You will need his help and understanding more than anything else.

Take care, however, when you seek advice and assistance. People tend to hold strong beliefs about what is right for mothers and babies. Some people in your life may feel adamantly that you should not work—or that you should "get over it" and not let having a baby change you in any way. Filtering out their prejudices might be easy if you were sure of your own feelings. But at the moment you, like many other mothers at this juncture, may be fluctuating from confidence to confusion by the hour. You need to figure out what is right for you and your baby, and you need time in which to do it. Someone else's experience or beliefs, and any advice based on them, need not be a factor in your decision making. Welcome encouragement, not persuasion.

Combating Fatigue

Regardless of the duties you are now re-shouldering, your first responsibility is to stay as rested as possible. Luckily breastfeeding requires that you sit or lie down and relax several times a day, while accomplishing something important—feeding the baby. Even pumping, once you are comfortable with it, builds in at least two "time-outs" during your day in which you can immerse yourself in a pool of calm and purposeful idleness. Be sure that you get to bed as early as possible every night. Save errands for the weekend, and then do only the bare essentials. Skip doing all but the most necessary household cleaning and other chores for now. In short, you still need to take tender care of yourself. Not only do you deserve it, but staying rested is essential to avoiding breast plugs and infections.

> *A really helpful baby gift: a cleaning service for your first weeks back at work.*

Bringing your baby into your bed to sleep, if you have not already done so, can be a big help. This can save you from getting up or even waking completely several times a night. Sharing a bed also gives you and your baby seven to eight additional hours of physical contact per day, and, since you'll nurse more often with your baby right beside you, it guarantees a bountiful milk supply. If you are not keen on letting your baby sleep in the middle of your bed, drop one side of his crib and push the crib up against your bed. You can then reach over and bring your baby beside you to nurse and put him back without ever getting up. (Bolt the crib to the bed, if necessary, so that your baby cannot slip into the crack between the two.)

You might put your baby down for the night in his own bed (in your room or his), and, after he wakes for his first nursing, bring him to your bed for the rest of the night. This way he gets accustomed to sleeping in his own bed, so that a full transition may be easier when he is weaned and when you and Dad want your bed back to yourselves.

Many mothers report that middle-of-the-night nursings are their favorite times. It's so quiet and peaceful, and you and your baby seem like the only people on Earth. No one else needs you; there's nowhere to go; you can just be together.

If you find that you get less rest rather than more with your baby in your bed, you might have him spend the night in his crib but bring him into your bed to nurse when he wakes at about five or six o'clock in the morning. This way you can have a long cuddle, perhaps dozing for another hour or two, and your baby's day will begin with a good, long dose of Mom and her milk. You can also put a twin bed in the baby's room and use it to nurse on lying down.

Nursing provides another essential rest stop at the end of your working day. Nurse your baby as soon as you arrive at the sitter's house or the day-care center. See how he wriggles when he hears your voice, how he relaxes his body against your own and turns to nurse with comical determination. He needs this, and so do you. As soon as you are home, get a snack and a large glass of water or juice, and sit down for a long cuddle and a nursing. Better yet, lie down on the sofa and take a nap while your baby nurses.

If you have older children, you might give them a snack and spread a large quilt on the living room floor for a daily rest and cuddle hour instead of launching right into the usual dinnertime frenzy. Like your baby, your older children are more likely to play happily while you prepare dinner if they've had their time with you first. You may want to hire a neighborhood teenager to come over every afternoon and evening to help get dinner started and to do a load of laundry or two so that you can focus on your children.

Take life slow on weekends. Afternoon naps and early bedtimes on Saturdays and Sundays should be the rule for the first six months of nursing and working. At any time of day, nursing while lying down and napping is a perfect way to nurture your baby while getting the rest you need. Don't begin any major home improvement projects or restart your social life with a vengeance just yet. The time will come again when you can drive yourself harder. Right now you need to reserve your energy for taking care of yourself and your baby.

Pay careful attention to the quality of your diet now, too, just as you did in the early weeks. You need nutritious, high-protein snacks both at home and at the office, and lots of fluids. Limit the amount of fat in your diet, however, as it can cause chronic plugged ducts.

> *Keep a bag of trail mix in your desk at work, and a squeeze bottle of water close at hand all day long.*

Exercise will help you combat fatigue, too. You may feel too short on time and energy right now to sign up for aerobics classes, but a regular evening walk (with or without your baby) will help you sleep more restfully and give you more energy.

How Your Baby Adjusts

Sometimes we forget to take care of ourselves because we are so concerned with how our babies are faring. How will your baby adjust to your return to work? More easily the stronger your attachment, reveals recent research. The National Institute of Child Health and Human Development (NICHD) has identified the quality of the infant-mother attachment as the single element that enables a baby to thrive in day care and avoid developmental difficulties down the road. The NICHD researchers conclude, "A baby's attachment to her mother is the best measure of her social and emotional well-being."

Since you are a responsive mother who has learned to read your baby's cues, your intuition will be your best guide to how well your baby is managing. How does your baby *seem* after a couple of weeks or more of day care? Is she fussier and clingier than before? Or does she seem like her same wonderful self? Another sign to look for is a developing attachment between your baby and your sitter. Are they becoming truly fond of each other? If so, terrific! You have enlarged your baby's emotional world to include another consistently present adult caregiver.

One sign that your baby may not be settling in at day care is end-of-day reports from the caregiver on behavior that just doesn't sound like your baby's. Consistently unfamiliar behavior may be a sign that your sitter and your baby are not developing a comfortable relationship and that your baby may need another kind of care. One mother who began taking her baby to family day care when she was eight months old found that her usually merry baby sobbed all day every day until pickup time. At eight months, often a time of intense separation anxiety, this baby simply couldn't adjust to day care away from home. Her mother found a sitter who could come to her house for a few months, and the baby was able to adjust better. When the baby turned a year old, the mother tried family day care again, and this time the baby settled in happily.

Babies often become fussy and demanding the moment their mothers arrive at day care after work. The provider may unhelpfully interject at this moment that the baby "hasn't cried all day," unintentionally implying that she is in tears because her mother has come. In a way, the implication is correct. Babies often wait until they are with their mothers to express all the frustrations and other feelings that have built up during the day. They know they are with the one person who can meet all their needs, and therefore they feel free to express them. School-age children do the same thing. If your reunions after work are marked by fussiness and crying, it's because your baby has saved a day's worth of her expressions of need for the person who really matters—you.

Take care not to interpret normal developmental changes as signs that your attachment is being disrupted. Working mothers, along with the rest of society, tend to blame everything that goes wrong with their children on the fact that their mothers work. Understanding what your child is likely to do whether you are working or not can keep you from being hard on yourself. The fact is that most infant behavior is unrelated to the mother's employment and unaffected by it, *if* the mother and baby are well attached.

At three to four months, for example, babies suddenly notice how fascinating the world is. Sometimes nursing a baby at this distractible age can seem more like a wrestling match as your baby wiggles and turns his head away because he can't bear to miss what else is going on (babies with exciting siblings are especially prone to this behavior). Although this developmental stage will soon pass—a five- to six-month-old baby will nurse with more resolve—it often coincides with a mother's return to work, and she may take it as a sign that her baby is somehow rejecting her.

On rare occasions, likewise, babies will stage "nursing strikes" during which they refuse the breast completely. Nursing strikes can have a range of causes: Something in the mother's diet may be making her milk taste different or causing an allergic reaction, the baby's gums may ache from teething, he may have a thrush infection, the mother's milk supply may be low, or the milk may be slow to let down. All these problems are correctable, and usually a striking baby can be coaxed back onto the breast. Nevertheless, a working mother may mistakenly and painfully interpret her baby's pushing and turning away during nursings—or sudden refusal to nurse at all—as a rejection.

Teething can also be a source of stress for mother and baby. A baby can cut teeth at four months or even earlier, and experience all the side effects that may come along with teething—fussiness, drooling, chewing, appetite loss, and restless nights—for weeks before a tooth comes in. If such behavior coincides with your return to work, consider teething as a possible reason.

Separation anxiety also gives working mothers angst. Peaking at any time between eight and eighteen months, separation anxiety is a normal part of infant development, but it can make a baby's introduction to substitute care difficult for all involved. If your baby gets anxious whenever you leave her sight, take extra care in helping her to become familiar and comfortable with your provider.

Reverse-Cycle Feeding

One behavioral change in babies that *is* due to having a mother who's away all day is a reversal of day and night sleeping and nursing patterns. By the age of eight to twelve weeks, a baby *may* have settled into a predictable pattern like this: Awake and alert all morning, he nurses two to four times between waking and midday, takes a long afternoon nap, and is awake in the late day and early evening. After dinner he sleeps for four or five hours, wakes and nurses once, and then sleeps for another three hours. But when his mother goes back to work, and the baby begins spending six to eight hours a day in substitute care, his pattern may change. He may sleep part of the morning and all afternoon at day care. He may accept 8 ounces of expressed breast milk once in the middle of the day, but seems satisfied thereafter until his mother comes to pick him up. Then, *ta da!* He may be awake and alert all evening, wanting to socialize with his parents and nurse frequently. He may increase the number of times he wants to nurse from once or twice to three or four times a night. His mother may wonder, "Why doesn't he ever nap at home anymore? Why isn't he sleeping through the night the way he used to?" and (of course) "What am I doing wrong?"

In studying working mothers and their babies, Irene Frederick and Kathleen Auerbach found that many well-attached babies sleep for longer periods during their mothers' absence and are wakeful when their mothers are present. These babies simply shift their schedules to nurse frequently when their mothers are available, and consequently may not need to be fed more than twice during an eight-hour separation. "You and your baby are a dyad," says Kittie Frantz, a pediatric nurse practitioner and lactation authority, "and are so well connected that the baby has adjusted as your body is adjusting." The baby simply goes into low gear while waiting for you. This is the highest compliment a nursing baby can give his mother; it is proof of a deep attachment between the two.

If your baby sleeps a lot and drinks little while you're at work, he will want to make up the missed daytime feedings with evening, nighttime, and early morning nursings. This can mean that, just after your baby has begun sleeping through most of the night, he resumes nursing several times a night again. Mothers whose babies sleep with them hardly notice the difference. The mother is getting all the rest she needs, her baby can nurse all he wants, and both mother's and baby's needs for physical contact with each other are fulfilled. If sharing a bed is not an option for you, nurse as long and as much as your baby would like in the early evening and morning, as well as once at night. Expect your baby to stay up much later than he might have before. If your baby feels physically and emotionally satiated during these hours he may keep his nursing to a minimum during the hours you would really like to have unbroken sleep.

A reversal of your baby's feeding cycle should mean less pumping for you. As one mother explained, "It seemed that all of my children would rather just tough it out until I came home from work; they wouldn't take anything from a bottle." If you pick up your baby at day care to find, day after day, that he has not drunk all the milk you have left, you can adjust your pumping accordingly. You may even find that when your baby is five or six months old and has begun sampling solid foods, your stock of frozen milk will meet all your baby's daytime needs for breast milk, and you can quit pumping altogether.

If your baby keeps with his old cycle, this doesn't mean that you are not deeply attached to each other. Your baby is probably one of those wonderfully flexible souls who adapts to new situations without batting an eye. But if reverse-cycle feeding sounds good to you, because it means less pumping, storing, and transporting milk, you can encourage your baby by putting him to the breast more often during the evening and just before you go to bed, even if he is asleep. Babies are quite able to nurse when in the "active" phase of sleep, which constitutes approximately half their sleeping hours. Your baby probably won't wake up fully to nurse, and will go right back to sleep afterward. If you wake up in the middle of the night, have another brief, quiet nursing. Add one more to your morning routine. The more your baby nurses while you are together, the less milk you will need to leave with your day-care provider.

Pumping and Your Milk Supply

Pumping has a reputation for being an onerous burden, but once it becomes a part of your daily routine—and you are letting down your milk in response to its stimulation—it is hardly any trouble at all. Think of pumping as a respite and a time to focus on your baby no matter where you are or what else is going on.

Your milk supply is normally at its highest level in both volume and fat content in the early and midmorning and lowest in the late afternoon. Therefore, an early-morning pumping session, especially if your baby is still sleeping and you are quite full, will yield the most milk. A midmorning pumping at work will also be productive, while your afternoon session may produce just half the midmorning amount.

If you fall into a pattern of nursing and pumping similar to the one in the example ("A Typical Day of Pumping and Nursing for a Mother of a Four-Month-Old"), you will probably have at least 8 ounces of fresh milk for your baby each day. Remember, though, that every mother-and-baby pair is different. If your baby nurses more often than the baby in the example, or if you obtain a lot of milk during your morning pumping sessions, you may not need to pump in the afternoon at all. Your baby may soon sleep through the late-night nursing,

A Typical Day of Pumping and Nursing for a Mother of a Four-Month-Old

5:00 A.M. Nurse (and sleep).

6:00 A.M. Pump both breasts. Yield: 2 to 4 ounces, to be saved for the following day or take to day care that morning.

8:15 A.M. Nurse briefly at day care.

10:30 A.M. Pump for 15 minutes at work. Yield: 3 to 5 ounces.

3:30 P.M. Pump for 15 minutes at work. Yield: 5 to 7 ounces.

5:30 P.M. Nurse briefly at day care.

6:00 P.M. Nurse longer at home.

9:00 P.M. Nurse.

1:00 A.M. Nurse (and sleep).

5:00 A.M. Nurse (and sleep).

too (if she has reversed her cycles, though, she may keep it up for quite a while).

If your baby is starting a growth spurt and requires more milk than you are pumping, you can supplement your fresh milk with frozen. If you pump more than your baby consumes in a day, add the extra to your frozen stocks. In the example, the mother's breasts have been stimulated and drained seven times in 24 hours, enough to maintain her milk production at the level she requires. In general, during the first four to five months after birth you will need to stimulate your breasts once every three to four hours while you and your baby are apart to keep your milk supply from decreasing.

When your baby is four to six months old, and has grown as big as she is going to be without yet becoming interested in mashed bananas and applesauce, you are likely to be at your peak of milk production. Your baby will consume most of your milk at the breast, but your pumping is likely to be at a peak as well. During this period you will want to be sure to keep your own protein and fluid intake high—especially if you are simultaneously returning to work.

Your milk supply will vary over the course of a week. After nursing more frequently on the weekend, you may find yourself a little full on Monday morning. At the end of a work week, you may find that your milk production seems a little low by Friday night. "Near the end of the week," recalls one mother, "my milk supply would go down. I nursed in bed a lot over the weekend so that I could rest and sleep while she built up my milk supply. On Mondays I had more milk and needed breast pads, but my supply was back to normal on Tuesdays." You may be able to counteract the fluctuations somewhat by decreasing your fluid intake on Sunday night and drinking more fluids all day Friday. But you'll find that your body is wonderfully sensitive to your baby's changing needs. As one mother says, "My body always seemed to know when it was the weekend." If you will not be pumping, extra nursing on weekends may be vital for rebuilding your supply for the coming week.

> *The nursing-working mother's rule: "My baby gets a bottle when I'm not there, and breastfeeds when I am there."*

Your milk supply can be affected by catching a cold, missed meals, stress, and fatigue. Taking decongestants or estrogen-containing birth-control pills can also diminish your milk production. Pumping, however, will help you keep your production up despite these things. If none of these seems to be a factor, yet your supply seems to be decreasing, consider the cycling rate of your pump (see Chapter 5, page 99). It may be cycling too slowly—not sucking as frequently as your baby does—and therefore not withdrawing the milk as efficiently. Try varying the speed of your pump, if possible, to mimic more closely your baby's sucking pattern over the course of a nursing session. One mother whose supply seemed to be decreasing recalls, "I realized that my daughter's sucking pattern had changed recently, so I tried mimicking her nursing pattern with the pump. When my flow slackened during a pumping session, I ran the pump on slow for a minute or two. Then I set it back up to medium (or fast and then medium). This gave me a second, but smaller, let-down." It is easy to adjust the cycling rate with an automatic pump; you can also do this with a manual pump, although you'll have to expend more effort. If you are unhappy with your pump in general, a different type or model may be the solution. See Chapter 5, pages 98–105, for suggestions.

Combining Breastfeeding and Formula Feeding

If you have decided to combine formula and nursing, and dispense with pumping, be certain to nurse *at least* seven times each weekday until your baby is well-established on solid foods. Encourage long nursings, especially if it is hard to manage frequent ones. Nurse lying down so that you can rest and sleep while your baby is getting all the milk and skin-to-skin contact he needs. One way or the other, you will need at least 2 hours of nipple stimulation, let-down, and withdrawal per 24-hour period to maintain your supply, and 3 or more hours to increase it. Night nursing and frequent nursing on the weekends will help ensure that your milk production stays bountiful.

Combining formula feeding and nursing may be problematic, however, during a baby's periodic appetite spurts. Since formula takes longer to digest than breast milk, a sudden increase in appetite may not be apparent while the baby is at day care. At home, though, the baby will want to nurse a great deal more than usual. Because the baby's appetite seems satisfied at day care and unsatiable at home, you may assume that you can no longer produce enough milk to meet the baby's needs. And, because you are not pumping during the day, you'll take longer to build your supply. Even a temporarily inadequate milk supply can shake a mother's self-confidence. Understanding what is happening can help you weather such episodes, and frequent short nursing sessions on your days off will close the gap between your baby's increased appetite and your milk supply. But pumping during separations from your baby, if only for a day or two, is the best way to raise your milk production to meet your baby's increased appetite.

After a baby is taking a lot of solids, combining nursing and formula feeding becomes easier. Still, if you reduce the number of daily nursings your milk supply may diminish until the baby becomes frustrated at the breast. To keep him from rejecting the breast, you might have your caregiver feed him formula from a cup instead of a bottle.

If you are having a lot of trouble maintaining your milk supply, consider adding fenugreek to your diet. A traditional milk-increasing spice, fenugreek is most commonly used now as the flavoring ingredient in artificial maple syrup. Fenugreek is available in capsule form at health-food stores. Kathleen Huggins, author of *The Nursing Mother's Companion,* reports that mothers who take two to three capsules three times a day usually see an increase in the milk supply within one to three days (you may also notice that your urine acquires a distinct odor of maple). Fennel seeds, too, have been used by women for centuries to increase breast milk production, and make a tasty tea.

Leaking

Your milk may have stopped dripping and spraying months ago but now that you are back at work you may be dealing with leaking milk all over again. Your breasts may leak when they are very full because you haven't been able to nurse or pump on your regular schedule, or even when something reminds you of your baby. (One mother found that her milk let down whenever she stepped into the elevator to go home to her baby. After a while her milk let down whenever she entered an elevator for any reason, forcing her to stand with crossed arms when she rode in one.) Once you have established a pumping schedule, your body will adjust, and leaking shouldn't be a problem any longer. Meanwhile, wear nursing pads in your bra to absorb any leaked milk (see Chapter 4, page 51).

Stop a leak discreetly by pressing on your nipples with the back of your forearms or with your elbows.

You can stop a leak, when you feel your milk letting down, by gently pressing on your nipples until the let-down sensation subsides. Do this discreetly by crossing your arms and pushing the sides of your hands directly against your nipples and breasts to stop the milk flow. At your desk or a conference table, you can also put your elbows on the table in front of you and your hands under your chin and press the backs of your upper arms against your breasts.

A new product, the Blis Breast Leakage Inhibitor System, is now available at maternity and baby-supply stores. Designed to restrict leaking milk by putting pressure on the nipple, this product is a flexible molded plastic cup that can be tucked into your bra. A bump protruding from its center presses against the nipple to stop leaks. The Blis cup is not recommended for women who have sore nipples or are prone to mastitis or plugged ducts.

As long as the leaking continues (which varies greatly from woman to woman), wear clothes that will camouflage leaks. Printed fabrics are a good bet. You might also keep an extra jacket, sweater, or long scarf at your workplace in case you need to throw it on to cover any spots.

Pumping at Work

The ease or difficulty of pumping at work depends on the nature of your workplace and your own comfort with your decision to nurse and pump. Regardless of how your coworkers feel about having someone pumping her breasts nearby, try to keep a relaxed attitude. Without being ashamed or secretive, you can keep your twice-a-day activity to yourself (since the newest pumps are so small and so quiet, and their cases discreet, this is easier than it once was). If someone asks about your pump or your brief disappearances, tell the truth. Pumping and storing milk at work may raise a few eyebrows, but not nearly so many as you might fear. One mother found that her colleagues reacted with fascination. "They wanted to see the milk, asked if it hurt to pump, and wanted to examine the pump," she said. If someone does voice disapproval, brush off the comments as you would any intrusion into your private life. You have chosen to do this for your baby and yourself; no one else's opinion matters. In all likelihood, your proud example will enlighten your colleagues and encourage other working mothers to breastfeed, too.

You may have no problem letting down your milk in response to the stimulation of your pump. Or you may find that, although your milk flows easily into the pump at home, pumping at work is less relaxing and less productive. Persevere; in time you will learn to relax and withdraw all the milk you need. Suzanne Johannet, a family physician and nursing mother, suggests putting a sign on the door of your bathroom, conference room, or supply closet, that says, "Will be done in 15 minutes." Unlike a "Do not disturb" sign or no sign at all, this tells the curious and the impatient all they need to know. Then you can erase thoughts of what is happening outside the room and turn your mind to your baby.

Set up a routine for pumping; it will calm your mind and help you to let down your milk. Begin just as you did at home when first learning to pump. Wash your hands and arrange your pump, pumping kit, and, perhaps, a picture of your baby in front of you. Keep a hand towel in your pump's carrying case to catch drips. For the first few days back at work you might bring along the shirt or sleeper your baby wore the night before, so you can breathe in his scent to stimulate your let-down. If it helps, you might imagine hearing your baby nursing, guzzling, murmuring, or even crying to be fed. You might hum lullabies, and lightly stroke your breasts with your fingertips. When you are relaxed and ready, fit the pump flange to your breast and turn on the pump. If you are using an automatic pump, begin with a slow cycle, and gradually increase the speed to medium or high. If you are using a manual pump, gently pump a few times until you feel your milk letting down, then hold the pump in its extended position and let your milk spray into it.

If you are using a single-side pump, switch your pump to the other breast when the spray slackens, and then back again. Switching back and forth will yield more milk than doing each side once. With a good let-down you may be able to collect as much as an ounce a minute. Strive to stimulate two let-downs per session.

Double-pumping—pumping both breasts at once—will probably yield more milk with less time and effort. One study found that double-pumping increases women's prolactin levels, causing more frequent and stronger let-downs and greater milk yield. Double-pumping also reduces the time required to pump from 15 to 20 minutes to 8 to 10 minutes.

After you are done pumping, store your milk in a refrigerator, freezer, or cooler (see page 109). Rinse the pump parts that have been touched by milk with hot tap water, and put away the pump. Later, at home, you can wash the parts more thoroughly with hot, soapy water.

(Daily boiling of all washable pump parts is not necessary unless so stated by the manufacturer. The rubber gaskets soon become dry and cracked with repeated heating, thereby reducing the pump's suction.)

As you keep up your pumping sessions, you will find that they become easier and easier, requiring less and less preparation and time and yielding more milk. Eventually pumping should take so little effort that you will be able to read or, with a one-handed pump, write or talk on the phone while pumping. At this point, your 15 minutes of pumping need not take you away from your work.

If you simply can't pump at work and you don't want to use formula, try pumping before your baby wakes in the morning and after her bedtime. You may be able to provide all the milk she needs in this way, or at least keep her formula feedings to a minimum. If your commute and schedule allow, see if you can visit your baby at lunchtime to nurse—or have your baby brought to you at work, and nurse in the middle of the day. A grade-school teacher whose husband worked at home and took care of their baby relied on this plan. Not only did her husband come by with the baby at noon every day so that she could nurse in the teacher's lounge, but he brought her a freshly packed lunch as well.

As your baby gets older, you may be able to reduce the frequency of your pumping sessions without compromising your milk supply. At some time during the second half of your baby's first year, you may wish to eliminate pumping altogether. As long as you nurse frequently at home, you may continue to produce the milk your baby needs. (You can let your baby have formula, water, or juice along with solid food while at day care. Note that pediatricians concerned about allergic reactions recommend that all babies be a full year old before receiving cow's milk.) Many working women breastfeed part time for as long as they and their babies desire, often right through toddlerhood, enjoying the closeness and intimacy of being part of a nursing couple despite the daily separations.

Transporting Your Milk

You do not need to freeze your milk as soon as you pump it, but you might want to keep it cool if hours are going to pass before it is drunk or frozen. Since bacteria counts in breast milk kept at room temperature actually go down, thanks to all the protective white cells circulating in the milk, you could safely leave the milk out until you head home. But if your workplace is especially warm, if your commute is long and hot, or if leaving your milk out just makes you fret, then cool it. You can put your milk in the freezer section of the company refrigerator, if there is one, so that it is half frozen by the time you leave work. If your drive is a short one, you won't need to insulate the milk in transit. Or skip freezing your milk altogether. Chill your bags of milk in the company refrigerator until the end of the day, then put them into a wide-mouth insulated bottle with crushed ice at the bottom for the ride to day care. Or put your pumped milk directly into the cooler compartment of your pump carrier, or into a separate small cooler or insulated lunch bag with a freezer pack.

Once you arrive at day care, leave your (labeled) milk in the refrigerator to stay cool until your baby's lunch the next day.

Teaching the Caregiver about Breastfeeding

Your baby's caregiver will be handling your expressed breast milk even more than you will. Even if she breastfed her own children, she may have little or no experience with storing and thawing breast milk. Copy the guidelines for safely storing and using fresh, frozen, and thawed milk (in Chapter 5, page 109), and give them to her.

If your caregiver is familiar only with formula-fed babies, you will need to explain that breast milk is digested much more completely and more quickly than formula. Exclusively breastfed babies, especially very young ones, may therefore want to eat smaller but more frequent meals than the formula-fed babies to whom she may be accustomed— although if your baby reverses his cycles he may take a bottle less often than the formula-fed babies. Day-care providers understandably need to organize their days, and scheduled feeding times are usually a part of that organization, but your baby is accustomed to being fed whenever he is hungry. Talk to your caregiver about this; be sure that she is willing to give your baby a bottle of expressed breast milk whenever he seems to want it.

Explain that one of the benefits of breastfeeding is that breastfed babies excrete less waste than formula-fed babies. Sometimes caregivers are surprised by the stools of breastfed babies. They are loose, yellowish or greenish, and mild, almost sweet, in odor—not at all like what one might find in the diaper of a formula-fed infant.

Also explain that breast milk looks different, and thinner, than cow's milk or formula. Breast milk can look bluish when fresh, and turns pale yellow when frozen. Explain that when it is left to sit, it will separate; the cream will rise to the top. Explain that the caregiver should shake the bottle to mix in the cream before feeding the milk to your baby.

If the caregiver will be using frozen milk, ask her to thaw only as much as she thinks she will need at a time. Thawed milk is less stable than fresh and will spoil if left at room temperature all day. If the caregiver is going on an all-day outing with the children—to the playground, perhaps—she can take along a bottle of fresh milk, which will keep much longer than thawed milk.

Show the caregiver how to thaw breast milk by letting the frozen bag sit in a cup of hot water for 15 minutes—and be sure she knows never to microwave breast milk. Let her see how you open a disposable bottle liner or freezer bag of thawed milk, pour it into a feeding bottle, and shake it to mix in the cream. If you'll want your baby to have rich meals at times, show her how to make double-cream bottles (see page 112).

Talk to your provider about when and where you would like to nurse your baby each day. Does she mind if you nurse at both drop-off and pickup? Ask her to avoid giving your baby a full bottle just before you arrive in the afternoon, so that he'll be willing to nurse long and well as soon as you get there. (For the times when your baby is hungry and you're stuck in traffic or in a late meeting, it's a good idea to keep a few 1- to 2-ounce containers of milk in the caregiver's freezer. If he seems very hungry, she might give him a double skim-milk feeding.)

Ask your caregiver to help you to keep track of how much milk your baby is drinking so that you can pump accordingly. Tell her about growth spurts (see page 48), and explain that she can draw on your frozen stores during those times—and that you'll value her judgment about how much more milk to provide.

Be sure that your caregiver understands that even on the hottest day of the summer your exclusively breastfed baby does not need water in addition to breast milk. Your breast milk provides him with everything he needs until he is at least four months old. As your baby grows and begins to add solids to his diet, your caregiver should know that she can use breast milk, just as she might use formula for another baby, to mix with cereal or applesauce.

Finally, remind the caregiver that your baby may strenuously object to drinking on his own from a propped bottle. As much as possible, your baby's substitute caregiver should nurture your baby as you do. Not only do you want your baby to be fed in arms, but to be picked up when he cries and carried when he needs the comfort of being close to another human being. Consistency in care will help your baby adjust to your separations with a minimum of stress.

Preventing and Treating Plugged Ducts and Mastitis

Plugged ducts and breast infections do plague some mothers. An employed mother is most likely to experience them during her first month or two back at work. Her milk is suddenly not being withdrawn as consistently or as well as it was during her maternity leave. She may be stressed and fatigued.

In one survey of nursing mothers, one-third reported that a period of fatigue and stress had preceded their mastitis. The rule for the mother of the newborn also applies to the mother recovering from a plugged duct or breast infection: if you're standing, then sit; sitting, then lie down; lying down, then sleep. And be sure that you are getting all the nutritious food and vitamins you need. For further advice on preventing and treating plugged ducts and mastitis, see pages 53–56.

HOW TO TREAT PLUGGED DUCTS OR A BREAST INFECTION

- Take off your bra, and go to bed.
- Nurse as much as the baby is willing, starting on the affected breast. Position the baby with her chin pointing at the sore spot.
- Apply warm compresses, and massage your breast toward the nipple.
- Drink plenty of fluids.
- If you have a fever lasting 24 hours or more, call your doctor. You may need antibiotics.

Staying Close to Your Baby

Missing your baby will probably be the hardest part of going back to work. Your first full day without your baby may be truly wrenching. But you can draw comfort from your breastfeeding relationship, which is proof that you and your baby are indispensable to each other. Each pumping session at work will remind you of this. Remember, too, that intensely missing your baby is a sign that you are well attached, and that therefore your work cannot distance you emotionally from your baby.

Just as your baby needs to be both physically and emotionally satiated by breastfeeding and contact with you, you need your full dose of your baby each day. As long as you are not working extraordinarily long hours, you make up for the missed hours at home by nursing, carrying your baby in a sling or baby pack, and socializing with her. Letting your baby sleep with you can dramatically increase the close contact between the two of you, making the hours that you are apart much easier to bear. When you're at home, concentrate on understanding and answering your baby's needs rather than fostering her "independence." Staying in harmony with your baby will make the separations less difficult, and your work may soon become a comfortable part of your routine.

As your baby grows and develops over the amazing first year of her life, so will you continue to grow and develop as her mother. Stay sensitive to the changes within you. Find ways to integrate the lessons you are learning as a mother into the other parts of your life, and wear your motherhood with pride. After spending several years helping to launch an exciting new publishing company, a distinguished editor and writer decided to return to her independent work. Addressing the staff at her good-bye party, she declared that being a part of the launch had been "one of the grandest adventures of my life, one matched only by being a mother." Appreciate your own grand adventure through motherhood, and garner the rich awards it can give you.

The lessons of breastfeeding in particular, can linger long beyond weaning. Most important, breastfeeding teaches the subtle but valuable lesson of receptivity. As Karen Pryor writes in *Nursing Your Baby,* "Think of the difference between 'passive' and 'receptive.' There is partnership implicit in being receptive that is the very nature of the nursing relationship." Approaching your family members and the people with whom you work with the receptivity you have learned through breastfeeding, as a *partner* open to their cues, will enrich your relationships. Trusting yourself as you have trusted that your body can nourish your baby will make every new challenge less daunting. The intuition that guides you in caring for your baby will thus serve you well in all areas of your life, if you let it.

Business Travel

If your job requires you to travel at some point during the first year after your baby's birth, you do not need to wean your baby. If your trip comes before your baby is four or five months old, consider taking him along. Will you be in meetings all day? The hotel you stay at can help you find a sitter. Do you have friends or family in the area to which you're traveling who can care for your baby while you work? Or can your husband, mother, or friend come with you? If your trip is to a large city or resort area, he or she and the baby can take in the sights while you work. Meetings at most conferences last two or three hours, with just enough time in between to run up to your room, or meet your husband, mother, or sitter somewhere, and nurse the baby. Bringing someone along to help you with the baby will add substantially to the cost of your trip, but will make it considerably easier. If bringing the baby along would scandalize your employer, just don't publicize the fact that you're doing it. The presence of your baby in your hotel room is not going to affect your performance in the conference room or the exhibit hall.

You might even wear your baby while you work. If you can do this with confidence, meeting your baby's needs without interrupting other activities, your only barrier may be the necessity of keeping up a "professional image." Perhaps you will be among the growing number of women who are inventing a new professionalism that incorporates the presence of contented babies and cooperative children.

Unfortunately, many business trips require 12- to 15-hour days of intense concentration and hard work. If you are meeting new clients, making sales pitches, or visiting laboratories or factories, bringing your baby along probably isn't an option, no matter how confident you are. The ease of traveling without your baby depends on how old he is and how much milk your body is making. If you are leaving a baby who is less than four or five months old, you will need to make your trip as short as possible, for both his sake and yours. He is probably still nursing seven or more times a day and will require a stored milk supply of at least 32 ounces per day. You may wish to supplement with formula, if your baby will drink it, so that your frozen stocks are not used up all at once. However, providing for a two-day separation could be the best use of your stored supply.

You will need to pump your milk nearly as often as your baby nurses to avoid becoming uncomfortably engorged with milk. You might be surprised to learn how much milk you are making, and how engorged you can become, when your baby is not there to remove it. Pack an effective portable pump, and find a way to take pumping breaks once in the early morning, twice during the day, and at least twice at night. Arrange your schedule to allow for these breaks, just as you would schedule in any other appointment. Pumping on a long plane trip may be the stiffest challenge of the trip. Airplane bathrooms barely have enough room to accomplish the purpose for which they are intended, much less for setting up a pump and expressing milk. Ask your husband or a friend to see you off, and nurse your baby in the airport if possible. If your flight is five hours or less, you can probably wait until you reach your destination before pumping. If you are going to another country and have a very long flight in front of you, bring along a hand pump. You may wish to practice with it beforehand, since hand pumps can be frustrating to use if you haven't learned how. A cylinder pump or an Ameda-Egnell One-Hand pump is a good choice for small spaces, since these pumps need not be set on a table to operate, can be tucked into a purse, and can be rinsed out with hot water in a small sink.

You may wish to discard your expressed milk (as wrenching as this can be) to simplify matters, rather than worrying about adequate refrigeration while you are on the move. If you want to save the milk you pump, you may wish to bring along a small picnic cooler, or invest in one of the coolers made especially for expressed breast milk, so that you can transport a large quantity of milk easily. One mother packed her milk in blue ice and sent it home by overnight delivery each day.

When your baby is older than six months, traveling becomes somewhat easier. Your baby may be supplementing his breastfeeding with solids and nursing less or not at all at night. You may still need to pump three or four times a day while you're away but are less likely to become engorged and uncomfortable.

Your milk production will probably decrease over the course of even a two- or three-day trip if your pump is inefficient or if you've pumped infrequently. Take a couple of days off work afterward, if at all possible, to be with your baby, nurse frequently, and build back up your supply.

Weaning

In most traditional societies, children are usually completely weaned somewhere between eighteen months and four years of age, but never before the end of the first year. American babies are rarely nursed beyond six months, despite the American Academy of Pediatrics' recommendation that all babies be nursed for a full year. Babies are weaned early in our society for many reasons, some of which are simply justifications for the fact that people are uncomfortable seeing an older baby or toddler still nursing. Many people, including medical professionals, assume that working women generally wean earlier than other mothers. In fact, the opposite is true. Working mothers who breastfeed tend to do so as long or longer than their at-home counterparts. Your baby need not wean any earlier than he might if you were not working.

If your milk supply was well established before you returned to work and began pumping, you should be able to produce as much milk as your baby wants indefinitely. Allow your baby to continue to nurse for comfort as well as for food, and breastfeeding will be a way for you and your child to reconnect after your separations for as long as you both wish. Nursing into the second year or longer offers significant emotional benefits to children as they begin to experience life's bumps and bruises.

When you do wish to wean, keep in mind that weaning is a significant developmental milestone, like crawling, walking, or eating solids, and that it rarely happens all at once. Sometimes parents treat weaning as if it were like quitting smoking. They try to follow a regimen that subtracts one nursing each week until the baby isn't nursing at all. But infants don't develop on a rigid schedule, and breastfeeding isn't an addiction. Watch how your baby progresses through other developmental stages. Milestones are almost always reached gradually with two steps forward, then one step back. This is why parents often recognize their children's developmental progress only in retrospect.

Very occasionally a baby gives up nursing over the course of just a few days. Perhaps a new tooth or an earache has made her reluctant to nurse (or to eat anything); somehow, when she is feeling better, she and her mother have moved on to a stage of life that does not include nursing. Or a baby may come to prefer the bottle because her mother's milk supply is low, although she would prefer nursing if she could get a good meal out of it. Or a baby might suddenly refuse to nurse because of something in her mother's diet that is making the milk taste odd or is causing an allergic reaction, or because of thrush or another infection. In all these cases, weaning may not be the baby's intention, but it happens anyway. Often her mother has seized the opportunity to wean her baby quickly.

Ideally, a nursing relationship evolves gradually over the course of six months or more into one that is just as close but in which breast-feeding is no longer a part. When this happens, neither mother nor baby may remember when they nursed for the last time. The mother may realize that her baby, whether one year, eighteen months, or two and a half years old, hasn't nursed for three or four days. Perhaps he will want to nurse again in a week or so when he stubs his toe. She might let him, or she might distract him with a hug and a cookie. In another week or month, she realizes that he is truly weaned. In most cases of gradual weaning, a mother uses gentle encouragement and creative substitutes for nursings as the baby becomes interested in other things.

Mothers as well as babies benefit from gradual weaning. Sudden weaning may bring with it an emotional letdown, by ending all at once the production of the nursing hormones and their soothing effects. Sudden weaning may even lead to serious depression, perhaps when the abrupt end of lactation causes an overload of minerals in the bloodstream. Gradual weaning helps avoid these effects.

Weaning also requires adjusting to the loss of the rest times that come with nursing—the excuse to lie down with the baby and relax. If your baby is very active, you may miss the physical intimacy of nursing, especially as your baby becomes a busy toddler with little time for cuddling. And weaning means losing your automatic cry-stopper; you will have to find other ways to comfort your baby as he grows. All of these changes are easier to adjust to when they are gradual. Over time, you can replace nursing breaks with quiet times spent napping or looking at books together.

If you wish that your baby would hurry things up a bit, however, you are not alone. No matter how much a woman has enjoyed breast-feeding, a time comes when she is ready to move on to the next stage of mothering. If you feel ready to be done with nursing, you can encourage gradual weaning. If your baby is less than a year old, you can probably substitute bottles or cups for nursings. If you would like to reduce or eliminate nighttime nursings and your baby is sharing your bed, it may be too much to ask her to give up night nursing and bed-sharing all at once. Spend a few nights sleeping in another bed while your baby stays in your bed with your spouse. If she cries for you, see if she will be satisfied holding your breast instead of nursing while sleeping in your bed. When she is out of the habit of nursing at night, gradually move her to her own bed.

If you are weaning a child one year old or older, choose a nursing that seems to matter less to your baby than others during the day, and casually substitute a cup of milk or juice (a choice between chocolate milk and a nursing can work wonders with toddlers).

Postponing a nursing works well for some toddlers. Ask your child to wait for his morning nursing until you get to the day-care provider's house, where he may be swept up in the day's activities and forget all about nursing.

With these gentle distractions, you can reduce nursing to the one per day that really matters to your child, probably the bedtime or early-morning nursing. This last nursing may linger for several months. At bedtime your husband may be able to help by putting your baby to bed for a couple of weeks, until he has forgotten about his end-of-the-day nursing. If the baby screams for you, Dad might try taking him for a walk or drive at bedtime in hopes that he will fall asleep on the way.

The Nursing Mother's Guide to Weaning by Kathleen Huggins and Linda Ziedrich, is full of wonderful suggestions for coaxing your baby to wean when you are ready.

Falling Apart

Sometimes, between six months and a year after her baby is born, a mother may feel herself falling to pieces. Although in the eyes of everyone else she has managed beautifully, she feels as if she cannot manage another second. After all, she is working or on call 24 hours a day. All her activities and most of her thoughts are dedicated to meeting someone else's needs. Her day is scheduled to the last minute. She hasn't found more than 20 minutes to herself in the last week, and when she says so people assume she is exaggerating. One evening she may find herself in tears, confessing to her husband or a friend on the phone that she "can't do it anymore. I cannot meet another need. I cannot take on one more responsibility."

In addition, just when she has got used to caring for a newborn whose needs—"feed me, change me, hold me, love me"—may have been constant but were relatively simple, she now has an older baby with a mind of his own, and the increasing mobility to satisfy it. Now Mom's on her feet as the baby explores everything he can reach with grasping hands and open mouth. She thought she had completed the adjustment to motherhood, but at six months she realizes that there is yet another stage to traverse—and yet more after this one are stretching into the distance.

The realities of motherhood have sunk in with a thunk. Yes, your life has changed irrevocably. It will get easier, but for the time being acceptance, rather than resistance, will help you to cope. Now that you are a mother, you can't flop down on the sofa with a magazine when you get home from work anymore. You can't be sure that your plans won't be thrown into the air like a deck of cards at the last minute because your baby has a fever or because the day-care provider unexpectedly closes her doors for the day. You aren't in total control of your life—and you won't have as much control as you'd like until your children are grown.

Although at-home mothers can also fall apart six months to a year after their babies are born, working mothers tend to find this time especially challenging. Dr. Sirgay Sanger, co-author of *The Woman Who Works, The Parent Who Cares,* points out that women in managerial positions especially "are used to being in control at work, and, like all parents, have to come to terms with the fact that children aren't controllable; they're their own persons." Lack of control is frustrating and worrisome.

You can learn, however, to ride out crises and other unpredictable events with flexibility and a sense of humor. This takes practice and an open mind, but the ability to say, "Ah, well—let's move on to plan B (or D, or Z)," or even, "Let's make it up as we go along," will serve you well at home and at work. Breastfeeding teaches this lesson well. (While learning to nurse, how many times did you say, "Well, if this position isn't working today, let's try another," or "Gee, I thought you were full; but if you would like to nurse again, that's fine"?)

Lack of time for yourself goes hand in hand with feeling out of control. It would be easier to be flexible if you could just get a break once in a while. Find ways to increase your efficiency and simplify your life at home (see "Managing Life at Home") so you'll have more time to do what you like. The working mother may actually have more oppor-tunities for building in time for herself than many at-home mothers. She has a daily lunch break—as much as an hour (what riches!) to do whatever she wants. Many working mothers confess that one of the joys of coming to work is being able to go to the bathroom whenever they want, *alone* and with the door *closed.*

If the six-month crisis hits you, find other mothers with whom you can talk. They know that you aren't exaggerating when you say you had only 20 minutes to yourself last week. With support from your friends, that end-of-your-rope feeling may be a brief though intense phase in your adjustment to motherhood.

Or your distress may compel you to reevaluate the decisions you have made about working. Perhaps you don't want to work full time after all. Reread pages 120–22 for ideas on redesigning your job to better fit into your life. More and more people are doing this; maybe you can, too. Whether a passing phase or a true crisis, feeling like you're falling apart is always a signal that you need to take care of yourself before you can take care of anyone else.

Managing Life at Home

"How," you may ask, "can I add taking care of myself to my list of responsibilities when I am already overwhelmed?" At home, search out ways of taking five- to ten-minute breaks. Deborah Shaw Lewis, au-thor of M*otherhood Stress,* writes that these mini-vacations are "golden moments, and they are almost always unexpected. You may not be able to plan them, so you have to watch for them. Suddenly you realize the baby is asleep, the kids are all playing a game, or there is absolute silence in the house. Take advantage of that. Consciously relax your body and say to yourself, 'Hey, I'm on vacation.' "

Try not to let your favorite pastime—gardening, playing music, hiking—languish during this busy first year. You can still do many such activities whether your baby decides to take a nap or not. Just put her in a sling or a baby pack and carry on. One mother plays her piano every evening while her six-month-old sits in a backpack looking over her shoulder, spellbound by her mother's dancing fingers and the won-derful sounds they make.

Look for every opportunity to do two or more things at once. Clean the kitchen or fold laundry while talking on the phone (cordless phones are a big help). While waiting at the post office, the gas station, the pharmacy, or in the grocery line, make a to-do list or a shopping list, balance your checkbook, write a postcard, or update your calendar. Do some stretching while your baby and any older children play in the park. While wearing your baby in a sling or baby pack, cook dinner, talk on the phone, fold laundry, or pick up around the house. If you use a computer, you may be able to get a lot of work done while wearing your baby. Your baby may be just as fascinated by your fingers on a keyboard and the flickering dots and lights of your computer screen as the baby of that pianist is fascinated by her playing.

As satisfying as it is to find ways to increase your productivity, you must also allow yourself to *decrease* productivity. Worrying about all the things you should do will wear you down. If a bed is left unmade or an errand not run, forget about it. The bed is going to be slept in again very soon, anyway. You can probably run the errand later in the week. Notice how often you tell yourself, "I should be doing this or that," and stop yourself from thinking it. You are not doing "this or that" now, and if it becomes a real priority then you *will* do it . . . maybe.

Simplify. List your activities and responsibilities for an average week. Which ones can you eliminate, share with someone else, or move to a more convenient time? Screen calls on your answering machine. (If you do pick up the phone and the caller wants to sell you something, say you don't buy anything from telephone solicitors. With luck, you will be taken off the lists of prospects, and in time your phone will ring less.) Keep a chalkboard or hanging pad of paper in a regular place so that you, your husband, and any older children can jot down household supplies that are running low. Check the list before you run errands or go grocery shopping. Use a milk delivery service, if there is one in your area. Sometimes butter, eggs, bread, and other basics can be delivered along with the milk. Invest in a large freezer to store precooked meals or prepared foods.

Appreciate the amount of work you do. How many of the following jobs are you primarily responsible for in your household? Cleaning the house, picking up daily clutter, bathing the baby, washing the dishes, arranging for babysitters, making doctor's appointments, driving children to school and day care, cooking meals and packing lunches, buying clothes for the family, feeding pets, gardening and watering houseplants, doing the laundry and taking clothes to the dry cleaner, grocery shopping, keeping medical and financial records, keeping tabs on items running low, paying bills, buying stamps, planning menus, organizing play dates, opening and responding to mail, staying in touch with adult friends, and making social plans for you and your spouse. Most or all of them, right? You can probably even add a few duties to this already breathtaking list.

The problem with the work of motherhood is that so much of it is invisible, especially when it is done well. Besides your happy and healthy children, there is no product to show for your efforts, and very little recognition for them. And yet mothering is hard, constant work. Write a list of the jobs you do—the baby care, the household chores, and the paid work—and read it whenever you feel you aren't getting anything done. It will remind you how much you really do accomplish. Consider posting the list on the refrigerator so that others, especially your mate, will see all that you put into keeping the house and caring for the family. How many of these responsibilities can he take over?

Finally, learn to live in the moment. The years when your children are little pass quickly, but leave deep imprints in both you and your children. Savor these days while you are living them. All too soon your babies will be grown.

> *"It is good to have an end to the journey towards; but it is the journey that matters in the end."*
>
> —URSULA LE GUIN

Managing at Work

Becoming a mother may make you ruthlessly efficient at work. After all, you cannot hang around the office until seven or eight o'clock putting the finishing touches on a project or chatting with colleagues. The efficiency you are learning at home will spill over into your paid work and help you finish tasks in less time. Office chitchat becomes less of a distraction and instead a rare indulgence.

The daily schedule of a working mother can be tyrannical. If you are not out the door and on your way to the babysitter's by 7:45, you will be late for work (again). You have exactly fifteen minutes to travel from work to day care or else you will be late to pick up your child (again). Many mothers find that their chief source of stress is all the times when the corners don't quite meet—when, for example, they have only five minutes instead of fifteen to make it to day care. Those five minutes, if they turn into twenty minutes in traffic, can alone deliver a full day's worth of strain and pressure. Other people can intensify such pressure. If you've left a late-running meeting early to arrive at day care ten minutes late, you may endure negative reactions on both ends.

Try to estimate realistic time requirements for every stage and transition in your day, and then pad your estimates. Other people may want you to be where they wish when they wish, but *you need to command your own schedule in order to minimize each day's stress.* If at all possible, arranging a flextime schedule at work is an ideal way to achieve this autonomy. Don't apologize for leaving while others are staying late; just explain that you must be at day care on time. Hiding the facts of your motherhood isn't good for you, your baby, or your coworkers. Work out a flexible arrangement with your day-care provider so that being five to ten minutes late *once in a while* will not upset her. Offer to pay for these extra minutes, even if you don't end up using them. You need to focus on your baby during your departures and arrivals at day care, not on conflicts between you and your provider.

Although you may be more efficient and doing better work than ever, you may find that you are still being taken less seriously than you once were. Perhaps this is because you leave at 5:00 sharp or because you have begun working on a flexible or part-time schedule. Your pumping breaks may leave more of an impression on the minds of your coworkers than someone else's slipping out to smoke a cigarette. Perhaps people automatically doubt your commitment to your job because you are now a mother.

You can counteract any perceptions that you may not be working as hard as you once did, without submitting to the urge to camouflage your motherhood. Write a memo summarizing each project you complete, and put a copy on the desk of anyone even vaguely connected to the project. When something comes up at home that requires a change of plans at work, offer several solutions at the time you present the problem. If your baby is running a fever and must stay home from day care, call in during the day to discuss ongoing projects at work. If you know that you are going to be out for a few days, leave a stack of completed work in your out-box, and arrange for someone to cover your responsibilities while you are gone.

When you feel discouraged by the challenges of combining work and mothering, think about all that you are learning and gaining during this vigorous time of your life. Appreciate the ways that working is good for you and your family. First, it brings in essential income.

It also offers the satisfaction of completing projects (and receiving monetary rewards and public recognition for doing so), something that motherhood rarely offers. In addition, working enables you to socialize with other adults every day. Conversations with colleagues can be relaxing and fun, and are something at-home mothers miss a great deal.

Consider also the ways in which the work you do as a parent enhances the work you do for pay. Every businessperson could benefit from the lessons of motherhood. In fact, many popular management seminars teach lessons that could come straight from a mother's experience. Every seasoned mother knows how to use her time efficiently, to set priorities, to delegate authority, to listen, to motivate others, to cooperate, to handle crises calmly, and above all to be patient. Every experienced mother can do six or more things at once—and do them well. Anybody who has quizzed a child preparing for a spelling test, wiped down the kitchen counters and loaded the dishwasher, refereed a sibling squabble, answered the phone, mentally run through the errands to be done the next day, made a grocery list, kissed a toddler's stubbed toe (and found the preferred cartoon-character bandage to put on it), and noticed that the dog needs water—all within the same 15 minutes—is well prepared for a high-pressure job. Dive into this demanding period of your life. You will emerge stronger and more able than you ever thought possible.

When Your Baby Is Sick

Waking up on a weekday morning to find that a child is running a fever or throwing up and cannot go to day care is a dreaded event for working parents. Many couples will "split the day" when a child is suddenly sick, one heading off to work as early as possible and coming home at noon so that the other can leave and stay as late as he or she needs to. You might be able to take your child into your office long enough to pick up paperwork or phone messages that you can take with you and handle at home.

Your backup caregiver may or may not be able to step in. A day at Grandma's house might be a perfect solution, but these days Grandma is probably heading out the door to her own job. Some cities have day-care centers designed especially for sick children. But it is hard to imagine a baby or toddler being very happy when dropped off at a totally unfamiliar place full of strangers, especially when he isn't feeling well. When a child is sick he very much wants his parents, especially his mother, with him. A breastfed baby feeling under the weather may be consoled by nothing but nursing. A sick older baby may give up solids for a few days and temporarily obtain all his calories from breast milk.

When your child is suddenly sick, try to keep your perspective. Yield to the situation. Take the day off to hold and nurse your baby. If he is fighting an infection, he will need the extra nursing and cuddling to get better as quickly as possible. (If your benefits include sick days for yourself and not for dependents, talk to your company about changing the policy so that parents don't have to lie to stay home with their children.)

> *"Setting my priorities and being true to myself has given me peace of mind, if not always happiness. Apologize to no one; it's your life."*
>
> —A MOTHER

Under any circumstances, don't dose your baby with Tylenol and send her to day care because "she is just going to sleep most of the day, anyway." Your baby may have caught the bug from another child at day care, but your provider needs all the help she can get in controlling the passing of germs among the children for whom she cares. Parents who knowingly bring sick children to day care are the bane of day-care providers.

If your child needs you at home for an extended period, and his need puts your job at risk, you may be able to take advantage of the federal Family Medical Leave Act, which requires employers with 50 employees or more to allow 12 unpaid weeks off for any employee who needs to care for a dependent. (You may not be entitled to this leave, however, if your request falls in the same calendar year as your maternity leave did.) Smaller companies are not required to comply with the act, but if yours is very dependent on you it may be willing to work out a temporary leave, flextime schedule, or work-at-home arrangement until the crisis passes.

Bringing Your Baby to Work

What about bringing your baby to work with you? If you work in a factory, hospital, laboratory, store, or restaurant, this may not be possible. But if you work in an office, bringing your baby along with you may be an option if she has a fairly innocuous but contagious illness like conjunctivitis or if she is well but her caregiver must take a day off. At a minimum, you might want to come in with the baby to pick up work to bring home and do while your baby naps.

You may, however, be able to get quite a lot of work done right in the office with your baby with you. If she is not very sick, just being near you may keep her happy most of the time. As at home, you can wear your baby in a sling, frontpack, or backpack while you do your desk or computer work. Or bring along a bouncy seat and a few interesting toys, and let her play at your feet as you work. Because you have encouraged a secure attachment since her birth, your baby is far more likely to play independently as long as you are near than would a baby who never gets enough of her mother.

Self-employed mothers with home offices are experts on blending work and mothering. Their experience offers practical ideas for every working parent. "As soon as my husband leaves, my baby and I 'get to work,' " says a freelance graphic designer. "If she's awake I put her on a baby blanket or in the frontpack, and use that time to talk on the phone to clients or suppliers. As soon as she naps, I go to my drafting table and do the work that requires creativity and intense concentration. I know that I can do certain kinds of work with my baby awake and other kinds only when she is asleep or with my husband. So I work around her schedule and am prepared to rearrange my plans whenever necessary."

A public relations specialist also arranges her work to harmonize with the rhythm of her baby's day. "I structure my time like this: Mornings when she is up and busy, I do lots of work on the cordless phone. After lunch it's naptime, and I sit at the computer and do work that requires concentration."

Breastfeeding streamlines baby care while you're working. A city planner advises, "As far as incorporating an eight-month-old into your work, I would suggest that this is much easier if you are breastfeeding. When my little one was tired of amusing herself, I could nurse her and continue to do whatever I was working on. I'm a great one-handed typist as a result!" She adds, "Now that my daughter is a toddler, I still bring her everywhere and hold her and cuddle her whenever possible. She's learned to join in if she can or to sit snugly on my lap, or in the sling when I'm occupied with work. It's the physical closeness that she really needs."

If your baby identifies your work as an opportunity to be close to you rather than an activity that takes you away from him, he is more likely to grow into a child who is happy to be near you while you work without demanding your undivided attention.

Blending Working and Mothering

"The key to combining work and mothering," says a writer and mom, "is not to set yourself up for failure—for anger at your child or yourself, for feelings of frustration and anxiety and guilt. Keep a list of what you've gotten accomplished, but not a list of ideal goals. The ebb and flow is more productive than you think." This is the secret— knowing that working with an "ebb and flow" rhythm is just as productive, and often more so, than dedicating definite chunks of time to particular tasks. The first is a distinctly feminine way of working, and the other is the way men tend to do things. But they are both valid, fruitful methods of working. Whether you can work productively while caring for your children depends on your attitude toward your work as much as how you keep your children busy and happy. Be flexible about when and how and where you work, and you may find that in the end you get as much done as if you had employed a rigid schedule and method.

A consultant to a nonprofit company points out that being a part of their parents' working lives benefits children. She says, "I suppose I've taken this to an extreme; my 28-month old son has been accompanying me to work since I returned to the office three months after his birth. It's been great on so many levels. I was able to breastfeed until we were both ready to stop; I have constant contact with my son and he with his mommy. He gets to experience different people coming into the office and see the way I interact with them, and he sees firsthand what I do—and now he can even help with some things!"

A landscape architect agrees that even young children can benefit from watching adults involved in productive work, "Children today are very isolated from the workplace. As a feminist, I have always thought that it was important for my children to see me at work. I have always brought them to meetings when I could, especially community meetings, so they will learn how to be involved in their community as they grow up." She adds, "My five-year-old, who is quite used to this, is very content to draw and color quietly and knows that Rule Number One is 'Don't interrupt Mommy when she's making a point!' "

Like the sons and daughters of farmers, shopkeepers, and other self-employed people through time, children who are integrated into their parent's working lives view themselves as more than dependents. They want to be partners in their parents' life work, contributing as much as their age and abilities allow. For these children, taking on their own responsibilities is as natural as learning to walk. For their mothers, work is not something that takes them away from their children—and their children don't take them away from work.

Revising your picture of how work and mothering fit into your life can make as much of a difference as revamping the ways in which you work. Mentally dividing your life into separate spheres—mother, wife, worker, friend, and self (with separate standards of achievement for each)—could lead to despair. You may feel that you are falling short of your own high standards in every one of your roles, or that success in one means failure in another. Perfectionism, though it may have gotten you wherever you wanted to go in the past, will let you down now. So trade it in for flexibility. Let motherhood, beginning with breastfeeding, teach you not to juggle, shuffle, or balance working and mothering, but to *blend* them.

CHAPTER SEVEN

CHANGING THE WORLD— ONE NURSING MOTHER AT A TIME

"I love my baby and I love my work. Why does one always tear me from the other?"

IN HER 1991 BESTSELLER *Backlash: The Undeclared War against American Women,* Susan Faludi sounded a clarion call to women to renew their commitment to feminism. Why have we been so hesitant to respond? Perhaps it is because we find, when we become mothers, that feminism lacks practical answers to the problems we face in our daily lives. Feminism has freed women to make choices, but it has thoroughly complicated the choices we make.

In the 1960s and 1970s, feminism asked women to downplay their differences from men—to fit into a workplace culture designed by and for men. Faludi explains why: "Examining gender differences can be an opportunity to explore a whole network of power relations—but so often it becomes just another invitation to justify them. Whenever the 'specialness' of women is saluted (or any population group's, for that matter), the recognition is bound to be double-edged. . . . Marking women as 'special' slips easily into demarcating limits on them. 'Special' may sound like superior, but it is also a euphemism for handicapped." When working women become working mothers they fear they will be discriminated against in the manner Susan Faludi predicts: They will be viewed as handicapped by their specialness. So they strive to prove their commitment to their employers by hiding their lives as mothers and never mentioning their children's needs. This has been hard on women—and especially hard on children.

The quandary faced by almost every working mother—the desire to be both recognized for her vocational abilities and free to meet her children's needs without apology or risk to her status—will not be resolved by masking her identity as a mother. The answer is to change our culture, to one in which baby care and child raising (and caring for all our dependents, including the elderly) are freely performed by all of society's able members. When nurturing is esteemed equally with achievement, then the lives of mothers and children will become infinitely easier and more satisfying.

This must be the next goal of women working to expand our opportunities. When we can employ our abilities publicly despite openly wearing this most womanly of emblems, motherhood, then feminism will truly have achieved its goals. Change begins with individuals. We can change the way our coworkers and managers perceive mothers in the workplace. Woman by woman, we can turn our culture into one that accepts the needs of children and enables mothers *and fathers* to meet those needs without penalty.

The first step is to overcome your company's prejudices that equate children with disruption, a lack of productivity, and unprofessionalism. You begin to accomplish this when, instead of trying to make your baby as independent from you as possible, you ensure that your attachment is deep and secure. Breastfeeding and caring for your baby in the ancient ways of working mothers can help you stay close to him emotionally, and thus better able to meet his subtlest needs. And a child whose needs are met is far less likely to be disruptive when his parent must focus on something other than him. A well-attached child is generally easy to integrate into the adult world. He is not a distracting burden, but an amiable companion to his mother. The more you show this to the people you work with, the less threatened they will feel by your commitment to your child, the less convinced they will be that children and work do not mix.

Whether you bring your child into work daily, occasionally, or not at all, be as open about your children and your life as a mother as you can be. Reject the notion that the image of a professional and the image of a mother are mutually exclusive. You know that your role as a mother does not impair your ability to do well at work. Your colleagues will know this too, if you let them. Find simple ways to remind them that you are a mother as much as an outstanding worker. Why not wear the bracelet your toddler made of pipe cleaners and plastic beads as part of your business attire? Frame your child's first work of art, and hang it alongside that diploma or award on your office wall. Keep crayons and baby rattles in your desk for any child who comes into your workplace.

Do not allow your coworkers and managers—or yourself—to devalue that part of you that is a mother. Instead, apply in your working life the qualities that motherhood teaches—empathy, cooperation, flexibility, trust in your instincts, calmness in crises, respect for the irrational, the ability to do several things at once, and the ability to loosen control temporarily without losing control entirely.

Open channels between you and other mothers in your workplace. Change the social climate so that they too begin to feel that they can be open about their motherhood without compromising themselves professionally. Again, simple actions can initiate significant changes. Bring in a garment that your child has outgrown: "Can you use this? It's too small for Sammy, and I hate to throw it away." Ask about others' children. Ask new mothers how they're doing and if there is anything you can do to help. If coworkers grouse because someone has left early to pick up a child, point out how productive that person is and how little time she spends chatting at the water cooler. Share information about breastfeeding and pumping. Once women shared a common body of knowledge about mothering. Now even at-home mothers are often isolated from one another, and working mothers especially miss out on the rich exchange of support and advice that makes raising children comprehensible rather than bewildering. A network of working mothers in your company can substitute for a neighborhood or extended family network, if you do not have either of those in your life. Sharing your parenting concerns will help you all to work better and with more enthusiasm—while staying close to your children. (By all means include fathers in your network, but don't be surprised if they don't understand the daily challenges you face as fully as women do. Most dads don't manage the minutiae of day care—packing extra clothes and diapers, remembering when day care is closed, making substitute arrangements, etc.—or schedule doctor's appointments and play dates, much less pump and transport milk.)

If you can change the social climate so that parents feel free to support one another, the status of mothers in your workplace may change dramatically. A company is far more likely to institute benefits and options for employees with dependents if requested to do so by a united group of respected employees.

Companies that are truly family-friendly offer a range of ways to work besides the standard five-day-a-week, nine-to-five schedule. Many of these corporations are leaders in their fields, in part because their policies attract the best and brightest employees. As Thomas Bouchard, a senior vice-president at IBM, writes, "Work/life issues are particularly important to our highest performers . . . [and] can have a direct positive impact on our ability to attract and retain a talented work force." Family-friendly policies, IBM understands, are good for business.

> *When* Working Mother *magazine created its first list of family-friendly companies in 1986, the researchers found just 30 firms worth recognizing. Ten years later, hundreds of employers competed to earn a spot on* Working Mother's *list of 100 best firms to work for. Perhaps in another ten years the list will be obsolete; family-friendly policies may be standard business practice.*

What policies and benefits would be most helpful to you, and worth fighting for if they are not already in place in your company? Flextime? A "phase-back" policy to allow new mothers to return to the workplace gradually? The right to use your sick leave when your child is sick? How about a three- or four-month maternity leave? With pay, even? Other family-friendly benefits that could make a real difference in your life are pretax set-aside payroll programs (your child-care costs would be deducted from your pretax income and paid to you separately as an untaxed benefit), and reimbursement for child-care costs associated with business travel and overtime work. On-site child care can be a dream come true or a disaster (what happens if your child is happy in the company day-care center and you decide to change jobs?). With a network of coworkers with children on your side, you may very well be able to realize your wish-list of benefits in your workplace.

At home, your husband's willingness to become an equal partner in running the household and caring for the children can do more than ease your workload. Don't let him assume that because you may take primary care of your baby, you should also have primary responsibility for household chores. Your ability to give birth and breastfeed does not carry with it an extraordinary talent at grocery shopping and laundry. Your husband can take as much or more responsibility for these chores as you do. And if he does, he will fully understand all the needs of your family and what must be done—and changed—in order to meet them. As more and more fathers understand what it means to be a truly involved parent and to keep a home, they too will bring change to their workplaces. Their dedication to their work is less likely to be questioned even when they are open about the needs of their families.

A vast change indeed is possible for our culture when individuals commit themselves to making it—and who is more committed than you, the nursing, working mother?

APPENDIX 1

RESOURCES FOR NURSING, WORKING MOTHERS

BREASTFEEDING SUPPORT GROUPS

La Leche League International
P.O. Box 4079
Schaumburg, Illinois 60168
800-525-3243 or 847-519-7730
Internet address:
www.lalecheleague.org
Call between 9:00 A.M. and 3:00 P.M. for breastfeeding help or a referral to a local La Leche group. A local phone number may also be listed in your phone book.

Nursing Mothers Counsel, Inc.
P.O. Box 50063
Palo Alto, California 94303
415-599-3669
Provides free mother-to-mother breastfeeding help through chapters in several cities. Call for a local phone number.

LACTATION CONSULTANT REFERRAL SERVICES

International Lactation Consultant Association
200 North Michigan Avenue
Suite 300
Chicago, Illinois 60601
312-541-1710
Call to locate a lactation consultant near you.

Breastfeeding National Network (Medela, Inc.)
800-835-5968
Call to locate a lactation consultant near you.

BREASTFEEDING SUPPORT SERVICES FOR BUSINESSES

Sanvita Programs (Medela, Inc.)
4610 Prime Parkway
P.O. Box 660
McHenry, Illinois 60050
800-433-5557
Provides help in establishing corporate pumping rooms and support for breastfeeding employees.

ELECTRIC BREAST PUMP RENTAL
INFORMATION

Medela, Inc.
4610 Prime Parkway
P.O. Box 660
McHenry, Illinois 60050
800-435-8316
Internet address: www.medela.com
*Provides referrals to local pump
rental stations.*

Ameda/Egnell Corporation
755 Industrial Drive
Cary, Illinois 60013
800-323-8750
*Provides referrals to local pump
rental stations.*

White River Concepts
924 C Calle Negocio
San Clemente, California 92673
800-824-6351
Internet address:
www.whiteriver.com

MANUFACTURERS OF BREAST
PUMPS FOR PURCHASE

*Ameda/Egnell cylinder pump,
One-Hand hand pump*
Ameda/Egnell Corporation
755 Industrial Drive
Cary, Illinois 60013
800-323-8750

*Medela SpringExpress and
Medela Manual hand pumps,
Mini-Electric pump, and Pump
in Style electric pump*
Medela, Inc.
4610 Prime Parkway
P.O. Box 660
McHenry, Illinois 60050
800-835-5968 or 800-435-8316

Nurture III electric pump
Bailey Medical Engineering
2020 Eleventh Street
Los Osos, California 93402
800-413-3216

*Other manual and battery-
operated pumps are available in
pharmacies and baby-supplies
stores.*

BREAST MILK COOLERS AND
CARRIERS

*Medela Cooler Carrier and
Medela Lactina Cooler Carrier*
Medela, Inc.
4610 Prime Parkway
P.O. Box 660
McHenry, Illinois 60050
800-835-5968 or 800-435-8316
*The Medela Cooler Carrier costs
about $20 and includes room for a
small battery-operated or manual
pump. The Lactina Cooler Carrier,
about $30, includes room for the
Lactina pump.*

Cool 'n Carry Tote
Ameda/Egnell Corporation
755 Industrial Drive
Cary, Illinois 60013
800-323-8750
*Includes room for a small battery-
operated or manual pump. Costs
about $25.*

BREAST MILK FREEZER BAGS

Mother's Milk Storage Bags
Breastfeeding Support Network
2050 West Ninth Avenue
Oshkosh, Wisconsin 54904
414-231-1611
*For 25 bags, $5.50 plus $1.00
shipping.*

Mother's Milk Freezer Bags
Ameda/Egnell Corporation
755 Industrial Drive
Cary, Illinois 60013
800-323-8750
*For 20 bags, $8.55 plus $3.00
shipping.*

Medela CSF Bags
Medela, Inc.
4610 Prime Parkway
P.O. Box 660
McHenry, Illinois 60050
800-835-5968 (for referral to a
local source)
800-435-8316 (to order direct)
*For 20 bags, $10.95; for 50 bags,
$18.95. If you order direct from
Medela, include $4.00 for shipping.*

VARIOUS NURSING SUPPLIES

Avent America, Inc.
1765 West Cortland Court
Unit A
Addison, Illinois 60101
630-495-0110
*High-quality bottles and breastfeed-
ing products.*

Baby Love Products
5015 Forty-sixth Street
Camrose, Alberta
Canada T4V 3G3
403-672-1763
*Large selection of pregnancy and
nursing products.*

Bosom Buddies
212 Broadway
P.O. Box 1250
Port Ewen, New York 12466
914-338-2038
*Nursing bras, breast pumps, and
milk cooler-carriers, as well as 100
percent cotton bedding for infants.*

**Mother Nurture: Everything for
Breastfeeding Guide and Catalog**
916 Royal Blackheath Court
Naperville, Illinois 60563
630-420-4233
*Breast pumps, milk cooler-carriers,
baby carriers, nursing bras and
clothes, and sewing patterns.*

Motherwear
320 Riverside Drive
Northampton, Massachusetts 01060
800-950-2500 or 413-586-3488
*Baby carriers, pumps and milk
coolers, breast pads, books, pillows,
and more.*

CLOTHES FOR NURSING MOTHERS

Mother Nurture: Everything for Breastfeeding Guide and Catalog
916 Royal Blackheath Court
Naperville, Illinois 60563
630-420-4233
Nursing bras and clothes, and sewing patterns.

Mother's Work
1309 Noble Street
Sixth Floor
Philadelphia, Pennsylvania 19123
800-825-2268 or 215-625-9259
Maternity and breastfeeding clothes for professional women.

Motherwear
320 Riverside Drive
Northampton, Massachusetts 01060
800-950-2500 or 413-586-3488

The Natural Baby Company
816 Silvia Street, 800 B-S
Trenton, New Jersey 08628
800-388-2229 or 609-771-9233
Nursing clothes as well as shaped and pinless cloth diapers and diaper covers.

BABY CARRIERS

Sling-Ezee
Parenting Concepts
P.O. Box 1437
Lake Arrowhead, California 92352
800-727-3683 or 909-337-1499

BabySling, Cuddle Me front pack, and Hug-a-Bye hip carrier
NoJo
22942 Arroyo Vista
Rancho Santa Margarita, California 92688
800-541-5711

The New Native Baby Carrier
P.O. Box 247
Davenport, California 95017
800-646-1682
This sling comes in various sizes according to the size of the parent.

POSTPARTUM SERVICES

National Association of Postpartum Care Services
P.O. Box 1012
Edmonds, Washington 98020
800-453-6852
Call for a referral to a local doula.

Doulas of North America
1100 Twenty-third Avenue East
Seattle, Washington 98112
206-324-5440
Call for a referral to a local doula.

Depression after Delivery
P.O. Box 1282
Morrisville, Pennsylvania 19067
800-944-4773 or 215-295-3994
Call for an information packet or a referral to a local support group.

CHILD-CARE SERVICES

Child Care Aware
1319 F Street N.W.
Suite 606
Washington, DC 20004
800-424-2246 or 202-393-5501
Provides referrals to local agencies that list licensed child-care providers of all kinds according to zip code.

ORGANIZATIONS SERVING WORKING WOMEN

Nine to Five: National Association of Working Women
231 West Wisconsin Avenue
Suite 900
Milwaukee, Wisconsin 53203
414-274-0925
This organization of office workers operates a Job Survival Hotline (800-522-0925). Trained job counselors respond to questions about flexible schedules, maternity leave, and balancing work and family.

Association of Part-Time Professionals
7700 Leesburg Pike
Suite 216
Falls Church, Virginia 22043
703-734-7975

Mothers' Home Business Network
P.O. Box 423A
East Meadow, New York 11554
516-997-7394
Dedicated to helping mothers work at home, this network offers its members a newsletter,
Homeworking Mothers.

F.E.M.A.L.E.
Formerly Employed Mothers at the Leading Edge
P.O. Box 31
Elmhurst, Illinois 60126
630-941-3553
A national, nonprofit organization for women who have left the full-time paid workforce to raise their children at home, F.E.M.A.L.E. helps women deal with the transition between paid employment and at-home motherhood. (Approximately 40 percent of F.E.M.A.L.E. members do work for pay, most of them part time.) F.E.M.A.L.E. advocates for choice in how one combines working and parenting.

Executive Options, Ltd.
910 Skokie Boulevard
Suite 210
Northbrook, Illinois 60062
708-291-4322
An employment agency that places professionals in part-time and short-term positions.

Catalyst
250 Park Avenue South
Fifth Floor
New York, New York 10003
212-777-8900
A national nonprofit organization that works with businesses to effect change for women through research, advisory services, and publicity.

Families and Work Institute
330 Seventh Avenue
New York, New York 10001
212-465-2044
Internet address:
www.familiesandwork.org
This nonprofit organization serves as a national clearinghouse for

information on issues concerning work and family, and develops educational programs and materials on these issues for government and business.

New Ways to Work
785 Market Street
Suite 950
San Francisco, California 94103
415-995-9860
Conducts research and provides information on alternative work arrangements, and promotes flexibility in the workplace.

Work/Family Directions, Inc.
930 Commonwealth Avenue
Boston, Massachusetts 02215
617-278-4000
One of the oldest consulting firms concerned with work and the family, this company provides research, strategic planning, and nationwide child- and elder-care referrals. Its Family Resource Program provides employees of client companies with advice on handling conflicts between work and family.

On-Line Resources

Web sites and message boards change frequently; however, the sites listed here are fairly well established. They provide links to sites on specific topics such as breastfeeding, working mothers, and attachment parenting.

The Femina Directory
www.femina.com
A "comprehensive, searchable directory of links to female-friendly sites and information on the World Wide Web."

WWWomen
www.wwwomen.com
This search directory for topics of concern to women also offers women's news, a help desk, chat rooms, and more.

ParentSoup
www.parentsoup.com
Maintains discussion groups, articles, and chat rooms on topics of interest to parents.

ParentsPlace
www.parentsplace.com
Includes bulletin boards, chat rooms, shopping, and articles on breastfeeding and other topics of interest to parents.

ParentTime
www.parenttime.com
Provides e-mail access to experts on breastfeeding and other topics, chat rooms, articles from TimeLife publications such as Parenting *and* Baby Talk, *and shopping.*

FamilyWeb
www.familyweb.com
Includes detailed discussions of breastfeeding, pumping, and day care as well as pregnancy, birth, and other topics of interest to parents.

RECOMMENDED READING

MAGAZINES

Birth
Blackwell Scientific Publications
3 Cambridge Center
Cambridge, Massachusetts 02142
617-876-7000

Mothering
P.O. Box 1690
Santa Fe, New Mexico 87504
800-984-8116

The Mother Is Me
P.O. Box 5174
Dover, New Hampshire 03821

The Nurturing Parent
3213 West Main Street
Suite 153
Rapid City, South Dakota 57702
800-810-8401 or 605-399-2990
www.thenurturingparent.com

Working Mother
135 West Fiftieth Street
Sixteenth Floor
New York, New York 10020
212-445-6100

BOOKS

Birth

Korte, Diana, and Roberta M. Scaer. *A Good Birth, A Safe Birth*, 3rd rev. ed. Boston: Harvard Common Press, 1992.

Breastfeeding

Huggins, Kathleen. *The Nursing Mother's Companion*, 3rd rev. ed. Boston: Harvard Common Press, 1995.

Huggins, Kathleen, and Linda Ziedrich. *The Nursing Mother's Guide to Weaning*. Boston: Harvard Common Press, 1994.

La Leche League International. *The Womanly Art of Breastfeeding*, 4th rev. ed. New York: New American Library, 1987.

Pryor, Karen, and Gale Pryor. *Nursing Your Baby*. New York: Pocket Books, 1991.

Baby and Child Care

Jackson, Deborah. *Three in a Bed: The Healthy Joys and Remarkable Benefits of Sharing Your Bed with Your Baby*. New York: Avon, 1989.

Jones, Sandy. *Crying Baby, Sleepless Nights*. Boston: Harvard Common Press, 1992.

Klaus, Marshall, and Phyllis Klaus. *The Amazing Newborn: Making the Most of the First Weeks of Life*. Reading, Massachusetts: Addison-Wesley, 1988.

Schulman, Michael, and Eva Mekler. *Bringing Up a Moral Child: A New Approach for Teaching Your Child to Be Kind, Just, and Responsible.* Reading, Massachusetts: Addison-Wesley, 1985.

Sears, William. *The Fussy Baby: How to Bring Out the Best in Your High-Need Child.* Schaumburg, Illinois: La Leche League, 1985.

Sears, William, and Martha Sears. *The Baby Book: Everything You Need to Know about Your Baby from Birth to Age Two.* Boston: Little, Brown, 1993.

Motherhood

Kitzinger, Sheila. *Ourselves as Mothers: The Universal Experience of Motherhood.* Reading, Massachusetts: Addison-Wesley, 1995.

LaMott, Anne. *Operating Instructions: A Journal of My Son's First Year.* New York: Pantheon, 1993.

Roiphe, Anne. *Fruitful: A Real Mother in the Modern World.* Boston: Houghton Mifflin, 1996.

Rosenberg, Judith Pierce. *A Question of Balance: Artists and Writers on Motherhood.* Watsonville, California: Papier-Mache Press, 1995.

Sears, Martha, with William Sears. *25 Things Every New Mother Should Know.* Boston: Harvard Common Press, 1995.

Working Parents

Davidson, Christine. *Staying Home Instead: Alternatives to the Two-Paycheck Family,* rev. New York: Macmillan, 1993.

Hochschild, Arlie, with Anne Machung. *The Second Shift.* New York: Avon, 1989.

Laqueur, Maria, and Donna Dickinson. *Breaking Out of 9 to 5: How to Redesign Your Job to Fit You.* Princeton, New Jersey: Peterson's, 1994.

Sale, June Solnit, Kit Kollenberg, and Ellen Melinkoff. *The Working Parents Handbook.* New York: Simon and Schuster, 1996.

Weisberg, Anne C., and Carol A. Buckler. *Everything a Working Mother Needs to Know.* New York: Doubleday, 1994.

Families and Culture

Leach, Penelope. *Children First: What Our Society Must Do—and Is Not Doing—for Our Children Today.* New York: Knopf, 1994.

Leidloff, Jean. *The Continuum Concept: Allowing Human Nature to Work Successfully.* Reading, Massachusetts: Addison-Wesley, 1977.

Reynolds, Jan. *Mother and Child: Visions of Parenting from Indigenous Cultures.* Rochester, Vermont: Inner Traditions, 1997.

For Children

Schwartz, Amy. *A Teeny Tiny Baby.* New York: Orchard Books, 1994.

SAMPLE PROPOSAL FOR PUMPING SPACE

MEMO

To: Human Resources Manager/Personnel Dept.

FR: Your name (or the names of all nursing mothers employed by your company)

RE: Proposal for accommodations for the use of working, nursing mothers.

Currently, ____ staff members are the mothers of breastfed babies. In light of the number of women of child-bearing age employed by [company name], it is likely that we will have more breastfeeding employees in the future. These employees each require a few minutes one to three times a day and an appropriate place in which to pump milk for their infants' meals during their separations due to work.

Pumping milk proceeds with more ease and is accomplished in significantly less time when it is done in a quiet, private space equipped with a few necessary items, including—

- a small room with a door that can be latched or locked from the inside;
- a comfortable chair and a small table;
- an electrical outlet within five to six feet of the table.

The following items are not necessary, but can enhance the usefulness of the room:

- a sink and a small refrigerator;
- a telephone for employees who would like to make or receive business calls while pumping their milk.

Facilities currently available to nursing mothers consist of the women's restroom, which is not an appropriately sanitary facility in which to prepare infant food; the employee locker room, which does not offer the privacy that speeds the pumping process; and borrowed private offices, which may inconvenience the primary users of these offices. A dedicated space for the use of nursing mothers will resolve all these problems.

Supporting breastfeeding mothers benefits the company in several important ways:

- Breastfed babies are statistically healthier babies. Healthy babies require that their parents miss fewer working days than do babies who have frequent respiratory and gastrointestinal illnesses. In addition, healthy babies mean fewer medical expenses for self-insured corporations such as [company name].
- Employees whose children are healthy and happy are better able to fully focus on their professional responsibilities.
- Employees who are able to pump plenty of milk at work (because a convenient, sanitary, and private pumping place has been provided) do not need to leave work in the course of the day to nurse their babies at day care.

Support for nursing mothers is among the many diverse family-friendly benefits leading corporations across the country have instituted to secure a dedicated and loyal work force.

Thank you for your attention to this important issue. Please let me [us] know if you have any questions regarding this proposal.

SELECTED REFERENCES

Auerbach, Kathleen G., and E. Guss, "Maternal Employment and Breast-feeding: A Study of 567 Women's Experiences." *American Journal of Diseases of Children* 138:958–60.

Baumslag, Naomi, and Dia L. Michels. *Milk, Money, and Madness: The Culture and Politics of Breastfeeding.* Westport, Connecticut: Bergin & Garvey, 1995.

Bettelheim, Bruno. *A Good Enough Parent: A Book on Child-rearing.* New York: Random House, 1987.

Bowlby, John. *Attachment and Loss,* vol. 1. New York: Basic Books, 1969.

Clutton-Block, T. H. *The Evolution of Parental Care.* Princeton, New Jersey: Princeton University Press, 1991.

Driscoll, Jeanne, and Marsha Walker. *Taking Care of Your New Baby: A Guide to Infant Care.* Garden City Park, New York: Avery, 1989.

Ehrenreich, Barbara, and Deirdre English. *For Her Own Good: 150 Years of the Experts' Advice to Women.* New York: Doubleday, 1978.

Eibl-Eibesfeldt, Irenäus. *Human Ethology.* New York: Aldine de Gruyter, 1989.

Fildes, Valerie. *Breasts, Bottles, and Babies.* Edinburgh: Edinburgh University Press, 1988.

Frantz, Kittie. *Breastfeeding Product Guide.* Sunland, California: Geddes Productions, 1994.

Grams, Marilyn. *Breastfeeding Success for Working Mothers.* Carson City, Nevada: National Capital Resources, 1985.

Hufton, Olwen. *The Prospect Before Her: A History of Women in Western Europe.* Vol. 1, 1500–1800. New York: Knopf, 1995.

Kennell, John H., and Marshall H. Klaus. *Parent-Infant Bonding,* 2nd ed. St. Louis: C. V. Mosby, 1982.

Lawrence, Ruth A. *Breastfeeding: A Guide for the Medical Profession,* 2nd ed. St. Louis: C. V. Mosby, 1985.

Lawrence, Ruth A. *Clinics in Perinatology.* Vol. 14, no. 1, *Breastfeeding.* Philadelphia: W. B. Saunders, 1987.

Mohrbacher, Nancy, and Julie Stock. *The Breastfeeding Answer Book.* Franklin Park, Illinois: La Leche League, 1991.

Neville, M. C., and M. R. Neifert, eds. *Lactation: Physiology, Nutrition, and Breastfeeding.* New York: Plenum Press, 1983.

Newton, Niles, with Michael Newton and others. *Newton on Breastfeeding: Reproductions of Early Classic Works.* Seattle: Birth and Life Bookstore, 1987.

Riordan, Jan. *A Practical Guide to Breastfeeding.* St. Louis: C. V. Mosby, 1983.

Riordan, Jan, and Kathleen G. Auerbach. *Breastfeeding and Human Lactation*. Boston: Jones and Bartlett, 1993.

Saunders, Stephen, Julie M. Carroll, and Carol E. Johnson. *Breastfeeding: A Problem-Solving Manual*, 3rd ed. Dallas: Essential Medical Information Systems, 1990.

Tannen, Deborah. *Talking from 9 to 5: Women and Men in the Workplace: Language, Sex, and Power*. New York: Avon Books, 1994.

Thurer, Shari L. *The Myths of Motherhood: How Culture Reinvents the Good Mother*. Boston: Houghton Mifflin, 1994.

INDEX